Make your point

30 Discussion Topics for Students at Secondary Level

LG Alexander *and* MC Vincent

I keep six honest serving-men
(They taught me all I knew)
Their names are What
  and Why and When
And How and Where and Who
                    Rudyard Kipling

Longman

Longman Group Limited
London

Associated companies, branches and representatives
throughout the world.

© Longman Group Ltd 1975

All rights reserved. No part of this publication may
be reproduced, stored in a retrieval system, or transmitted
in any form or by any means, electronic, mechanical,
photocopying, recording or otherwise, without the prior
permission of the copyright owner.

First published *1975
Fifth impression 1978

ISBN 0 582 55509 4

Acknowledgements

We are grateful to the following for permission to reproduce
copyright photographs:

Barnaby's Picture Library for pages 7 bottom left, 15 bottom, 49
centre left and centre right; Camera Press for pages 27 left (photo
by Paul Almasy), 27 centre and right (photo by David Robinson);
Fox photos for page 7 top and bottom right; Keystone Press
Agency for pages 11 top, 21 bottom, 49 top left and bottom;
Mansell Collection for page 33; Radio Times Hulton Picture
Library for page 31; Syndication International for page 15 top.

We are grateful to the following artists:

Michael Davidson for pages 19, 39; Martina Selway for pages 1, 5,
13, 25, 51, 55, 57; Mary Tomlin for pages 3, 9, 11, 17, 37, 59;
Robin Wiggins for pages 35, 45.

Filmset in Hong Kong by T.P. Graphic Arts Services
Printed in Singapore by International Press Co (Pte) Ltd.

Contents

		page
	To the teacher	v
1	Who'll get the job?	1
2	The foolish frog	3
3	Farms or factories?	5
4	Boys' work, girls' work?	7
5	What's your verdict?	9
6	Down with football	11
7	Why are you late?	13
8	Focus on water	15
9	The boy who cried wolf	17
10	Beauty *and* brains	19
11	Too old at twenty	21
12	A good alibi?	23
13	Music or money?	25
14	Too much…too little…	27
15	Find the right job	29
16	Books belong to the past	31
17	Focus on success	33
18	Should school children take part-time jobs?	35
19	Why can't I do what I like?	37
20	Forget it?	39
21	Who makes the decisions?	41
22	The young scientist: cruel or curious?	43
23	What should schools teach?	45
24	Equal rights?	47
25	Motor vehicles—a blessing or a curse?	49
26	Foolish or fashionable?	51
27	What kind of mind have you got?	53
28	Focus on work	55
29	Examinations are a necessary evil	57
30	The school holidays are too long	59
	Answer page	61
	Some useful phrases	62

To the teacher

Basic Aims
The widespread interest in *For and Against* (an oral practice book for use with advanced students of English as a foreign/second language) has led to repeated requests for a similar book at an easier level.
Make your point has been written to meet this demand. Like its companion, *For and Against*, this book has two broad aims: the first is purely linguistic; the second is educational.

At a linguistic level this book sets out to meet the problems posed by the unstructured 'conversation lesson' by providing a flexible programme which the teacher can manipulate according to the needs of his class. *Make your point* can be used in a fairly mechanical way for guiding conversation in an unresponsive class, or conversely, it can be used creatively as a source-book for ideas in a highly responsive class.

Over and above this basic linguistic objective, *Make your point* is concerned with moral education and social values. Most of the topics deal with serious issues, though some are in a lighter vein (e.g. Nos. 6 and 12). They have been selected for their relevance to modern living and they deal with issues which are of particular concern to teenagers. The exercises are designed to encourage and train the pupils to think for themselves. In the course of discussion it is unlikely that pupils (or anyone else for that matter) will find the right answers to some of the problems posed, but at least they might be tempted to ask some of the right questions.

Whom the book is for
This book should be found suitable for:
1 Secondary school pupils at the intermediate level who are preparing for the Cambridge First Certificate in English examination. It may be used in addition to an intermediate course like *New Concept English*, *Developing Skills* or *Mainline Skills A and B*.
2 Secondary school pupils at the intermediate level who are not preparing for an examination of any kind and who are attending classes mainly to improve their command of spoken English.
Make your point has been designed specifically to meet the needs of secondary school pupils and will therefore NOT be found suitable for adult students.

A description of the material
Layout
Make your point consists of thirty lessons each of which is laid out on facing pages. A 'text' (the term is used in the broadest possible sense) always appears on the left-hand page while exercises to guide discussion always appear on the right-hand page.
Left-hand Pages: The 'texts'
Each topic for discussion is first presented through a 'text'. Each text

has been kept deliberately short and simple to enable the pupils to concentrate on conversation rather than comprehension. Every effort has been made to project each topic as vividly as possible so the style of presentation varies greatly from text to text. For instance, there are seven dialogues, three purely visual pages, and a variety of texts which includes picture stories, fables, letters, notes, maps, diagrams, etc. Where a particular style recurs, general cover titles are used. So some texts are labelled 'Focus' (i.e. on a problem), 'Forum' (i.e. general discussion) or 'Viewpoint' (i.e. expressing a personal opinion). Most of the 'texts' deal with vital issues. It is hoped that pupils will feel sufficiently motivated by each topic and the way it is presented to attempt to participate in a discussion.

Right-hand Pages: Guided Discussion

The right-hand pages generally fall into five parts labelled A, B, C, D and E. The five exercises are designed to guide the student from highly controlled discussion (closely based on the text) to the open-ended discussion of topics suggested by the text. Each exercise takes the following form:

A *Comprehension:* This section consists of questions which are designed to ensure that the *meaning* of the text has been fully established in the pupils' minds. In the early lessons the questions demand straightforward answers: e.g. negative/affirmative tags and responses to Wh-/How questions some of which can have more than one answer and can be spread round several pupils. The first five right-hand pages provide teachers with examples of most of the different kinds of questions that can be asked, as a guide for extending the oral work in the later lessons if necessary. The questions in the later lessons are more interpretative or open-ended. They are concerned with *implied* meaning.

B *Oral Composition:* The purpose of this exercise is to enable pupils to reproduce an argument they are familiar with and/or to construct an argument of their own with the aid of notes. This section, therefore, usually contains notes from which the pupils will:

1 reconstruct two sides of an argument;
2 reconstruct one side and make up the other;
3 construct both sides of an argument (as for example in the visual pages). Occasionally, the pupil is asked to take a stand and state his own case using his own words.

C *What's Your Opinion?* The rationale behind this section is to involve the pupil personally either by direct questions about what he/she likes/does or by direct invitation to comment on the topic.

D *Talking Points:* This section is designed to provide opportunity for more extended oral work (e.g. describe/talk about topics related to the text). At this point in the lesson pupils will participate in free conversation.

E *Conclusion:* This very brief section rounds off each lesson and gives the pupils something to think about or to do in their own time. The section may contain a quiz or a proverb or an assignment or recommended reading, etc.

Structural Grading
Left-hand pages: The texts have been carefully graded in terms of language content to follow four of the six stages given in the *Handbook to the Longman Structural Readers*. The texts become progressively more difficult, the earliest ones being written within the limitations imposed by Stages 3 and 4 of the Handbook, the final ones going beyond the limitations imposed by Stage 6. However, even though the texts become progressively more demanding, they are always brief enough to ensure rapid presentation in the classroom.
Right-hand pages: Lessons 1–25 are written throughout within the limitations imposed by Stages 5 and 6 of the Handbook, though the early lessons contain fewer difficult structures and lexical items than the later ones. The introduction of a broader range of structural and lexical items on these right-hand pages has been inevitable as open-ended discussion cannot be productively confined to the simpler levels defined by the Handbook. However, teachers should always remain aware of the fact that some of the structures and/or lexical items on these pages will need to be explained during the course of discussion. (All explanations should be brief, not laboured!)

The grading scheme as a whole may be summarised as follows:

Left-hand Pages
Lessons 1– 5: Handbook, Stages 3/4
Lessons 6–10: Handbook, Stage 4
Lessons 11–15: Handbook, Stages 4/5
Lessons 16–20: Handbook, Stage 5
Lessons 21–25: Handbook, Stages 5/6
Lessons 26–30: Open

Right-hand Pages
Lessons 1–25: Handbook, Stages 5/6
Lessons 26–30: Open

Time Allocation
Assuming a lesson of 50 minutes, the suggested time allocation is as follows:

Phases of the lesson	Approx. time in minutes
Presentation of text	5–15
A Comprehension Questions	5–10
B Oral Composition	5–10
C What's Your Opinion?	5–10
D Talking Points	5–10
E Conclusion	0– 5

The first phase, presentation, is very important since the whole lesson depends on it. A reasonable effort should be made to cover all the remaining phases during the course of a lesson. However, if a lively discussion develops in class after the presentation phase then the lesson will have achieved its purpose even if the exercises have only been partially covered or—in some instances—completely ignored. It will be found in practice that unresponsive classes will need to go through the exercises systematically while responsive classes will often be able to take short cuts.

How to tackle each phase
Presentation (5–15 minutes)
This will vary according to the type of text. Two forms of presentation are recommended:
1 Listening Comprehension
2 Interpretation

1 *Listening Comprehension:* This is recommended for all texts which lend themselves to this form of presentation: i.e. those which can be read through without interruption. These are as follows:

Dialogues:	Nos. 1, 3, 11, 13, 18, 23, 26.
Fables:	Nos. 2, 9.
Viewpoint:	Nos. 6, 16, 19, 30.
Picture Stories:	Nos. 7, 10, 20.
Total:	16 Texts.

The suggested steps in the presentation are as follows:
a Introductory Commentary (books shut)
b Listening (books shut) (books open in the case of picture stories)
c General Comprehension Questions (books shut)
d Intensive Reading (books open)
e Listening (optional) (books shut)
f Reading Aloud (optional) (books open)

In practice this would work out as follows:
a Introductory Commentary *(books shut)*: Say a few words about the subject matter of the text by way of introduction. (E.g. I'm going to read you a text/dialogue about . . .)
b Listening *(books shut)*: Read the text to the class straight through without pauses, explanations or gestures, The pupils *listen* only and try to understand as much as they can at first hearing.
c General Comprehension Questions *(books shut)*: Ask a few general questions about the main points in the text to find out how much the pupils have understood at first hearing.
d Intensive Reading *(books open)*: Read the text in small units (e.g. a sentence at a time or less) making sure the pupils really understand it. Rather than give direct explanations, it is best to try to get as much information as possible from the pupils themselves. (Think of it as a 'corkscrew operation'.) Explanations should be given in English, but this shouldn't be carried to absurd lengths.

If, despite an explanation, pupils still fail to understand, then translate briefly and move on.
e Listening (optional) *(books shut)*: Read the text straight through again. The pupils should listen only.
f Reading Aloud (optional) *(books open)*: Ask a few pupils to read the text aloud or to take parts in the dialogues and discussions.

2 *Interpretation:* This style of presentation is recommended for all texts which pose problems, require special study, invite personal involvement, etc. These are as follows:

Visual pages:	Nos. 4, 14, 25.
'Problem texts':	Nos. 5, 8, 12, 15, 17, 21, 22, 24, 27, 28, 29.
	(NB The first parts of Nos. 17, 21, 22, 27 and 28 could be used for listening comprehension purposes.)
Total:	14 texts.

The suggested steps in the presentation are as follows:
a Introductory Commentary (books shut)
b Intensive Reading and Interpretation (books open)

In practice this would work out as follows:
a Introductory Commentary *(books shut)*: Exactly as above.
b Intensive Reading and Interpretation *(books open)*: As above. However, it is not enough merely to communicate the meaning of each text: plenty of guidance should be given to enable the student to *interpret* the text as well. Ask questions to find out whether the pupils have understood the implied meaning as well as the direct meaning.

Once the presentation phase has been accomplished the lesson may proceed with reference to the exercises on the right-hand page.
A *Comprehension Questions (5–10 minutes):* Ask the questions listed in this section (even if similar questions have already been asked during the Intensive Reading). Supply additional questions of your own if you wish to. Try to ensure a rapid *pace*. In the case of unresponsive classes it may be necessary to extend this section considerably by asking all types of questions (e.g. those demanding tag answers.) Examples of the range of questions that can be asked are to be found on the first five right-hand pages.
B *Oral Composition (5–10 minutes):* Ask the pupils to refer to the numbered notes and explain particular difficulties (e.g. new words). Now ask two pupils to reconstruct the arguments or let the whole class join in by referring individual pupils to the numbered sections.
C *What's Your Opinion? (5–10 minutes):* Ask the questions listed and ask the pupils to refer to this section if necessary. This exercise may be conducted round the class or pupils may be asked to work in pairs: e.g. 'Nos 3, 7.' (It should be noted, however, that work in pairs generally has the effect of slowing down the pace of the lesson.)

D *Talking Points (5–10 minutes):* When you reach this section, ask the pupils to read the questions to themselves and give them a couple of minutes to think about the problems posed. Then guide the class into a discussion by asking each question. Pupils may need prompting by means of additional questions before a proper discussion can develop. If a pupil makes mistakes while speaking it is best not to interrupt him. When he has finished briefly point out one or two major errors he might have made. Some useful phrases for free discussion can be found on page 62.

E *Conclusion (0–5 minutes):* Conclude the lesson briefly by referring to this section. Some of the assignments may be set as homework.

It cannot be stressed too strongly that the 'set lesson' as outlined above can be abandoned altogether if a lively discussion is generated after the presentation of the text, or by any one of the sections.

Other possible uses

Though this book is primarily intended for guiding conversation, it may be put to a variety of other uses. Some of the texts may be found suitable for speed-reading or scanning: pupils may be asked to look rapidly through a text in a limited time to see if they can 'get the point' quickly and accurately. You may occasionally give dictation exercises or ask pupils to write argumentative compositions as homework following a classroom discussion. Written exercises of this kind may be found useful in consolidating aural/oral work done in the classroom. But it is important not to lose sight of the overall objective of the book as a whole, which is to develop discussion skills by presenting a range of topics which are, for the most part, of universal human interest and concern.

1 Who'll get the job?

Interview 1
Miss Draper Good morning. Do sit down. You're Anne Porter, aren't you?
　Anne Porter Uh-huh.
Miss Draper Which school do you go to?
　Anne Porter Mm..mm High.
Miss Draper I'm sorry. I couldn't hear you. Did you say Merton High?
　Anne Porter No, Burton.
Miss Draper What's it like?... Well, what's your favourite subject?
　Anne Porter I don't like any subject much, but I'm good at maths.
Miss Draper I see. Have you any hobbies?
　Anne Porter Not really.
Miss Draper What do you do in the evenings then?
　Anne Porter Watch T.V.
Miss Draper Why do you want to work in a shop?
　Anne Porter er...I don't want to work in an office.
Miss Draper Have *you* any questions for me?
　Anne Porter (Shakes her head)

Interview 2
Bill Baker Sorry I'm late. Good afternoon.
　Miss Draper Good afternoon. Please sit down. Your name's Bill Baker, isn't it?
Bill Baker Yes, that's right. I'm from Brent Boys' School.
　Miss Draper Have you a favourite subject?
Bill Baker Yes, I have—history, but I'm better at art. I'm no good at maths!
　Miss Draper What are your hobbies?
Bill Baker I like all sports. In the summer I swim a lot.
　Miss Draper What do you do in the winter then?
Bill Baker (laughs) I stay indoors. I'm making my own Hi-fi set.
　Miss Draper Why do you want a job in a shop?
Bill Baker I think I'd like it. My uncle has a radio shop...(etc.)

Who'll get the job?

Presentation 1

A Comprehension
1 What is Anne wearing?
2 She isn't smiling, is she?
3 Has she met Miss Draper before?
4 Does Anne speak clearly?
5 Are her answers long or short?
6 What's her best subject?
7 Is she a dull or a lively girl?
8 Do you think she is rude, or shy?
9 Was Bill punctual for his interview?
10 He looks untidy, doesn't he?
11 Does he look cheerful?
12 How does he answer the questions?
13 What's his worst subject?
14 When does he stay indoors? Why?
15 Why does he want to work in a shop?
16 What questions could he ask?

B Who'll get the job?
Here are Miss Draper's notes on the interviews:

a Say what she thought of Anne.
FOR
1 Was punctual, smart, tidy. Would look nice in a shop.
2 Good at Maths—would add up bills correctly.
AGAINST
3 Was very shy—spoke too quietly, didn't look at me. Seemed rude—didn't answer. Might be rude to customers.
4 Seemed dull—no hobbies; no questions about the job. Might not work well.

b Say what she thought of Bill.
AGAINST
1 Arrived late, looked untidy. Shop assistants must be smart.
2 Bad at Maths—might make mistakes in the bills.
FOR
3 Was very cheerful, friendly—smiled, answered questions fully. Spoke clearly. Customers would like him.
4 Showed interest—uncle has a shop; asked questions. Would work hard.

C What would an interviewer think of you?
Answer the following questions. Choose the letter that fits you best:
  a always   *b* usually   *c* often   *d* sometimes   *e* never
1 Are you smart and tidy?
2 Are you punctual?
3 Are you cheerful and friendly?
4 Do you speak clearly?
5 Do you like meeting people?
  Now check your score on p. 61

D Talking Points
1 What would you wear for a party/a picnic/an interview/a day's shopping?
2 When you go shopping, what do you notice about the shop assistants?
3 What can you learn about a person from his clothes?
4 Why are some people more shy/rude than others?

E Find out
about jobs in shops. How much are shop assistants paid? Which customers do they like/dislike? What hours do they work?

The foolish frog

Once upon a time a big, fat frog lived in a tiny shallow pond. He knew every plant and stone in it, and he could swim across it easily. He was the biggest creature in the pond, so he was very important. When he croaked, the water-snails listened politely. And the water-beetles always swam behind him. He was very happy there.

One day, while he was catching flies, a pretty dragon-fly passed by. 'You're a very fine frog,' she sang, 'but why don't you live in a bigger pond? Come to my pond. You'll find a lot of frogs there. You'll meet some fine fish, and you'll see the dangerous ducks. And you must see our lovely water-lilies. Life in a large pond is wonderful!'

'Perhaps it *is* rather dull here,' thought the foolish frog. So he hopped after the dragon-fly.

But he didn't like the big, deep pond. It was full of strange plants. The water-snails were rude to him, and he was afraid of the ducks. The fish didn't like him, and he was the smallest frog there. He was lonely and unhappy.

He sat on a water-lily leaf and croaked sadly to himself, 'I don't like it here. I think I'll go home tomorrow.'

But a hungry heron flew down and swallowed him up for supper.

The End

The foolish frog

Presentation 1

A Comprehension
1 Who once lived in a tiny pond?
2 Was it deep or shallow?
3 Were there any plants in the pond?
4 There weren't any fish, were there?
5 Which other creatures lived there?
6 Why was the frog very important?
7 He was happy there, wasn't he?
8 Who passed by one day?
9 What did she ask the frog?
10 Describe the creatures in her pond.
11 Was her life dull or wonderful?
12 The frog followed her, didn't he?
13 How did he get to the other pond?
14 Why was he unhappy there?
15 Where did he sit?
16 When did he decide to go home?
17 What happened to him?
18 Do *you* think he was a foolish frog?

B Two points of view
a State the frog's point of view.
   FOR   SMALL POND
1 Safe—could swim across it.
2 Important—everyone knew him; other creatures polite.
   AGAINST   LARGE POND
3 Dangerous—big, deep, strange.
4 Lonely—no one knew him; other creatures rude, unfriendly.

b State the dragon-fly's point of view.
   AGAINST
1 Dull—nowhere to go; nothing to see.
2 Boring creatures—snails, beetles; no fish, ducks. Small plants.
   FOR
3 Exciting—dangerous ducks.
4 Interesting—meet a lot of creatures; plenty to do, see.

C Would you rather go to a large school or a small one?
In a large school:
1 You work in a big building—get some exercise between lessons.
2 You have special rooms for different subjects—don't stay at one desk.
3 You can learn more subjects—there are more teachers.

In a small school:
1 You work in a small building—don't waste time between lessons.
2 You stay in your own classroom most of the time—don't lose things.
3 You can learn better—don't have different teachers every term.

a Are all these points true? Can you suggest any more? What's *your* opinion?
b Which type of school is better for young children/for pupils of your age?

D Talking points
1 Describe your first day at a new school. How did you feel?
2 Are there any dangers in your everyday life? If so, what?
3 Describe a visit to a strange place. Was it exciting?
4 Would you like to leave your home and travel abroad? Why/why not?
5 Does everyone want to be important? Would you like to be? Why/why not?
6 Do you know anything about real pond life? If so, tell us.

E A proverb
'One man's meat is another man's poison'. Try to collect some more English proverbs.

3 FARMS or FACTORIES?

Mr Hunter Gentlemen! Listen to me, please. I've come here to *help* you.
　Farmer Kent Oh no you haven't! You want our land.
Mr Hunter I want to build two factories. I don't need much land for that.

　Farmer Kent You'll take too much. And we don't want factories on our island.
Farmer Stubbs No, we don't. Factories are ugly.
　Farmer Binns They're noisy.
Farmer Dodds They're smelly.
　Mr Hunter *My* factories will give you work, and money.
Farmer Binns We've got work. We're farmers.

Mr Hunter How big are your farms? How much do you grow?
　Farmer Dodds We grow enough to feed ourselves.
　Farmer Stubbs It's a good life.
Mr Hunter A good life? You work every day of the week. You never have holidays.

Farmer Stubbs We don't need holidays.
　Farmer Kent You can't change our lives.
Mr Hunter But your lives *are* changing. Where are the *young* men? Why do they leave the island? Why do they go to the cities?

Farms or factories?

Presentation 1

3

A Comprehension
1 Does Mr Hunter live on the island?
2 Who is he talking to?
3 Are they friendly towards him?
4 What does Mr Hunter want to do?
5 He doesn't need much land, does he?
6 Will the farmers give him any?
7 Why don't they want factories?
8 How could factories help the island?
9 The farmers don't want to change their lives, do they?
10 Are they sensible or stupid? Why?
11 Where have the young men gone?
12 Can you suggest why?
13 Would factories bring them back?

B The arguments
a *State Mr Hunter's argument.*
 FOR FACTORIES
1 Will help the island—work, money; fixed hours, pay, holidays.
2 Don't need much land.
 AGAINST FARMS
3 Very small—don't grow much.
4 Long hours—no pay, holidays.
5 Young men don't like them—leave.

b *State the farmers' argument.*
 AGAINST
1 Will spoil the island—ugly, noisy, smelly.
2 Will take too much land.
 FOR
3 Belong to farmers; grow own food.
4 A good life—like hard work; don't want to change.

C Would you like to work on a farm?
1 Do you like working outdoors?
2 Could you get up early every day?
3 Do you like animals?
4 Are you strong?
5 Would you like to work by yourself most of the time?
If you answered 'Yes' to 3 or more questions, you'd like farming.

Would you like to work in a factory?
1 Do you like working indoors?
2 Would you like to work fixed hours?
3 Could you work with noisy machines?
4 Do you like working in a big group?
5 Could you do the same thing all day and every day?
You'd like working in a factory, if you answered 'Yes' to 3 or more questions.

D Talking points
1 Do you agree with the farmers or Mr Hunter? Say why.
2 Have you ever visited a factory/farm? If so, tell us about it.
3 Do you think it's important to have your own land? Why/why not?
4 Farms produce food. What do factories produce?
5 Are farmers' lives changing? If so, how?
6 What do country people want to do when they come to town?
7 When people from the town go to the country, what do they want to do?
8 Would *you* rather live in a town or in the country? Why?

E A problem
Throughout the world people are moving from the country to the towns. What difficulties does this cause? Name two or more. Is it wrong? How would *you* persuade people to stay in the country? Suggest ideas.

4 Boys' work, girls' work?

a Learning to cook

b Mending a puncture

c Learning to use a plane

Boys' work, girls' work?

Presentation 2

4

A Look at the photos

a Learning to cook
1 Was this photo taken in a home or a school? How do you know?
2 Are the pupils boys or girls?
3 Is the teacher on the right or the left of the photo?
4 Why are the boys wearing aprons?
5 What do you think they are making?
6 Are they enjoying the lesson?

b Mending a puncture
1 Who is older, the boy or the girl?
2 What's the boy doing?
3 Why isn't he helping the girl?

c Learning to use a plane
1 Is the girl doing needlework or woodwork?
2 Which hand is pushing the plane?
3 Do you think she likes the work?

B Boys and girls should learn the same things.

a State the argument FOR
1 Schools should prepare pupils for the future—men and women will be equal.
2 Both will look after the children. Both will work outside the home.
3 So boys and girls should learn the same things; everyone should learn cookery, needlework and woodwork.

b State the argument AGAINST
1 Men and women are different—women are made to have children and should look after them.
2 Men should look after women—earn money, do heavy jobs.
3 So schools should teach boys and girls different things—boys' work—woodwork; girls' work—cooking.

C What about you?

a Questions for boys
1 Can you cook?
2 Can you sew?
3 Do you help with the housework?
4 Could you look after a baby?
5 Do you think boys should learn to do these things? Why/why not?

b Questions for girls
1 Can you use a plane?
2 Can you saw wood?
3 Can you mend a puncture?
4 Could you put up a shelf?
5 Do you think girls should learn to do these things? Why/why not?

D Talking points

1 Do you think men and women are equal? Why/why not? Will they ever be?
2 Here is a list of jobs. Which do men do? Which do women do? Which do both men and women do? Can you explain why? Is it the same in all countries?
   shop assistant, doctor, secretary, nurse, sailor, bus driver, chef, teacher, journalist bank-clerk, engineer, dressmaker, pilot
3 Should boys/girls go to a school for boys/girls only, or to a mixed school? Which is better for younger/older children?

E Choose a present:

What would you give a boy for his seventh birthday? What would you give a girl? Why?

5

What's your verdict?

Last month game wardens caught a gang of poachers in Mgaba Game Park. They found 25 crocodile skins in their hut. The trial will take place next week. The lawyers have prepared their case. Here are their notes.

Counsel for the Prosecution

1 Poachers guilty—broke the law—no licence to shoot crocodiles.
2 Too lazy to get jobs.
3 Killing one of the oldest animals on earth—very rare now—our country must preserve crocodiles.
4 Tourists come to see crocodiles—if they disappear the country will lose money.
5 So not only poachers, but also traitors ∴ punish them severely.

Counsel for the Defence

1 Men innocent—don't understand new laws.
2 Have always hunted crocodiles—shows they're brave.
3 Crocodiles take their food—eat children etc.
4 No jobs in that district—everyone very poor.
5 Men are just tools—real criminals are in the city.
6 Businessmen buy skins cheaply—make expensive handbags etc. from them; sell them to actresses, film stars—big profits.
7 Wrong men are in court—send them home; help them.

5 What's your verdict?   Presentation 2

A What are the facts?
1 Who caught the gang of poachers?
2 When and where did they catch them?
3 What did they find in their hut?
4 When will the trial take place?
5 What have the lawyers done?
6 Is it against the law to shoot crocodiles?
7 Did the poachers have licences?
8 They haven't got jobs, have they?
9 Do they come from a rich district?
10 Are crocodiles rare or common now?
11 Why have men always hunted them?
12 Why do tourists come to see them?
13 Tourists spend money, don't they?
14 Who do the poachers work for?
15 Do the businessmen pay high prices for the skins?
16 What do they make from them?
17 Who do they sell their goods to?
18 Are their profits big or small?

B The lawyers' arguments
a Make the speech for the Prosecution.
1 Why are the poachers guilty?
2 Why haven't the poachers got jobs?
3 Why is it wrong to kill crocodiles?
4 What must the country do? Why?
5 What will happen if crocodiles disappear?
6 What else are the poachers?
7 What should the court do?

b Make the speech for the Defence.
1 Why are the men innocent?
2 What have they always done? Why?
3 Why haven't they got jobs?
4 Who are the real criminals?
5 What are the men from the park?
6 Why do the businessmen want skins?
7 Who should be in court?
8 What should the court do?

C What's your opinion?
1 If a man doesn't know the law and breaks it, is he innocent or guilty?
2 What's your verdict in this case? Are the men guilty of poaching?
3 Do you think the men are traitors? Why/why not?
4 Do you think the businessmen are the real criminals? Why/why not?
5 If you were the judge, what would you decide: a) to punish the men severely b) to punish the men lightly c) to send the men home and help them.
6 If these men are punished, will the crocodiles be safe? Why/why not?

D Talking points
1 What do you know about crocodiles? Have you ever seen one? If so, where?
2 Do people need crocodile bags, watch-straps etc.? Why do they buy them?
3 Many other wild animals are disappearing:—leopards, rhino, deer. Why?
4 Is it more important to save wild animals or to help poor people?
5 What do tourists come to see in our country? What do they buy?

E A problem
How can we save wild animals? Here are some ideas. Do you agree with them? Can you add any more? 1 Put all poachers in prison. 2 Punish the men who buy skins. 3 Put rare animals in zoos.

6 Viewpoint

down with FOOTBALL

says Betty Brown

Why do people play football? It's a stupid game, and dangerous too. Twenty-two men fight for two hours to kick a ball into a net. They get more black eyes than goals. On dry, hard pitches they break their bones.

On muddy ones they sprain their muscles. Footballers must be mad. And why do people watch football? They must be mad too. They certainly shout and scream like madmen. In fact I'm afraid to go out when there's a football match. The crowds are so dangerous. I'd rather stay at home and watch T.V. But what happens when I switch on? They're showing a football match. So I turn on the radio. What do I hear? 'The latest football scores'. And what do I see when I open a newspaper? Photos of footballers, interviews with footballers, reports of football matches.

Footballers are the heroes of the twentieth century. They're rich and famous. Why? Because they can kick a ball around. How stupid! Everyone seems to be mad about football, but I'm not. Down with football, I say.

11

Down with football

Presentation 1

6

A Comprehension
1 Does Betty Brown approve or disapprove of football? Why?
2 How does she describe a game?
3 In what ways is football dangerous?
4 What does Betty Brown say about footballers?
5 What's her opinion of people who watch football?
6 Why can't she escape from football when she stays at home?
7 Does she think footballers deserve to be heroes? Why/why not?

B Down with football! / Up with football!

a *State the case AGAINST football.*
1 Football—stupid, dangerous.
Footballers fight—black eyes; break bones; sprain muscles.
Must be mad.
2 People who watch—mad too.
Shout, scream; dangerous crowds.
Stay at home—football on T.V., radio, newspapers.
3 Footballers—heroes; rich, famous— kick a ball.
Stupid—everyone mad.

b *State the case FOR football.*
1 Football—sensible, healthy.
Better to fight on football pitches than in life.
More danger in homes, on roads.
2 Footballers—deserve fame, money— can't play when old; great skill; give pleasure to millions.
Football popular—matches exciting.
3 Everyone can't go to matches—T.V., radio, newspapers report.
Betty Brown is the mad one!

C What's your opinion?
1 Are *you* mad about football? Why/why not?
2 Why do people go to football matches: to watch a famous player, to support a team, to see the skill of the players, or to shout and scream?
3 Do you think there's too much football on T.V., radio, and in the newspapers? Why/why not? Do you think football crowds are dangerous?
4 Do you think footballers deserve to be rich and famous? Why/why not?
5 Do you think Betty Brown would enjoy watching football if she could play? Why do other women go to matches? Should women play football?

D Talking points
1 Have you ever watched a football match? What was it like?
2 Describe a famous footballer. How does he play? What's his life like?
3 Have you ever broken a bone or sprained a muscle? How did it happen?

E What's your score?
1 Pele is from   a Spain   b Argentina   c Brazil   d Italy
2 England won the World Cup in   a 1958   b 1962   c 1970   d 1966
3 The most popular sport in the world is   a tennis   b baseball   c cricket   d football

(Answers: see p. 61)

7 Why are you late?

Peter Where's my breakfast?
Mr White Your mother's ill. Go and phone the doctor. Quickly!

Peter He's coming.
Mr White Right. I'll stay here. You'd better get to school.

Peter (thinks) Oh dear, I'm late. What will Mr Jones say?

Mr Jones Ah, good *evening* Peter. Why are you late?
  Peter I missed the bus.
Mr Jones Get up earlier.
  Peter But my father...

Mr Jones I don't want any excuses. You're half an hour late, so you must stay for half an hour after school.
  Peter But my mother...

Mr Jones No excuses! You've broken a school rule. 'Pupils must not be late.' If I don't punish you today, the whole class will be late tomorrow.

Headmaster Oh Mr Jones. You teach Peter White, don't you?
Mr Jones Yes, I do. He's quite a good pupil, but he was late this morning.

Headmaster I can explain that. His mother's ill and has gone to hospital. His father's just phoned.
Mr Jones Oh dear. I'd better see Peter again.

Why are you late?   Presentation 1   7

A Comprehension
1 Did Peter have any breakfast?
2 Why hadn't his mother cooked it?
3 What did his father tell him to do?
4 Who waited for the doctor?
5 How late was Peter for school?
6 Do you think the lesson had begun?
7 What did Mr Jones say to Peter?
8 What did Peter try to tell him?
9 Why didn't Mr Jones listen?
10 Which rule had Peter broken?
11 Why did Mr Jones think he should punish Peter?
12 Who spoke to Mr Jones at break?
13 What did he tell him about Peter?
14 How did the headmaster know?
15 Was Mr Jones sorry to hear the news?
16 Do you think he'll forgive Peter?
17 What do you think he'll say to him?

B Should Mr Jones punish Peter?
a *Give the reasons FOR (before break)*
1 Peter very late—middle of the lesson.
2 Asked him why—missed the bus—thought he'd got up late.
  Began to make excuses—didn't listen.
3 Had broken rule; began to argue.
  Must punish boys who break rules—if I don't, everyone will be late.
4 Teachers must be firm.

b *Give the reasons AGAINST (after break)*
1 Headmaster spoke to me at break—Peter's mother ill.
2 Explains why he was late.
  Tried to tell me—didn't listen.
3 Usually a good pupil—punctual.
  Must be worried, unhappy—unkind to punish him; will see him again, talk to him.
4 Teachers should be kind, fair.

C Are you a good pupil?
1 Do you work hard?
2 Do you write neatly?
3 Do you get good marks?
4 Do you listen to your teachers?
5 Do you obey the school rules?
   Did you get 5/5? Excellent.

Would you be a good teacher?
1 Are you patient?
2 Are you kind?
3 Are you fair?
4 Can you explain things well?
5 Do you like hard work?
   If you got 4/5, you'd be good.

a Do you agree with these questions?
c What's *your* idea of a good pupil?

b Are these questions sensible?
d What's *your* idea of a good teacher?

D Talking points
1 Have you ever been late for school? What happened? Were you punished?
2 What are the rules in your school? What happens when you break them? Would you like to change any of the rules? If so, which ones and why?
3 If there were no rules and no punishments in a school, would pupils behave?
4 What kind of rules are there outside school? What happens to people who break them? When and why do we forgive them?
5 Do your parents ever punish you? Why? How? Are they always fair?

E Suggested Reading
'Tom Brown's Schooldays' by Thomas Hughes
New Method Supplementary Readers Stage 4 (Longman 1963)

8 Focus on water

What's this?
It *was* a river. But now you can't swim in it. It's too dirty. Fish can't live in it. There's not enough oxygen. All the water-birds have gone, and the plants have died. If you drank the water, you'd die too.

What's happened? Factories have poured waste into the river. They have poisoned the water with their chemicals. Clean water goes into the factories and poison flows out. We must stop this.

We want clean rivers

Focus on water

Presentation 2

8

A Comprehension
Look at the first photo
1 How many fish can you see?
2 Are they alive or dead?
3 How do you know?
4 Would you eat them? Why/why not?
5 Do the plants look healthy?
6 Why aren't there any water-birds?
7 Would you swim in this river?
8 Would you drink from it? Why/why not?
9 Can you see a bottle? How did it get into the river?
10 Why is the river so dirty?
11 What must we do? why? *Look at the second photo*
12 Do you think there are any factories near that river? Why/why not?

B Who makes the rivers dirty?
a *State the case against factories.*
1 Factories greedy, dirty, selfish—use gallons of clean water, chemicals. Waste contains chemicals—flows into rivers; poisons water.
2 Could clean their waste—don't—say it's difficult, expensive. Don't see dead fish etc. Don't care—only interested in profits.
3 Spoil rivers for everyone—can't swim, picnic, row.
Soon no water to drink.

b *State the factories' defence.*
1 Can't afford to clean waste—people won't pay higher prices—want cheap goods, not clean rivers.
2 *Everyone* makes rivers dirty. Farmers use chemicals—kill insects; grow better crops.
Families use chemicals—wash clothes, clean houses; drains go into rivers. Children throw rubbish into rivers.
3 Scientists will find new chemicals—clean rivers; use sea-water.

C How guilty are you?
1 What did you use water for last week? Did you waste any?
2 Have you ever thrown anything into a river or pond? If so, what? Why?
3 Do you swim, row or water-ski? If so, how dirty do *you* make the water?
4 Do you like hot baths, clean clothes? Would you give them up/pay more for them in order to keep rivers clean? Why/why not?

D Talking points
1 Is there a river near your home/school? If so, describe it.
2 What would happen if factories couldn't use chemicals?
3 What do *you* think we can do about dirty rivers?
4 Why can't we drink sea-water? What happens when oil gets into the sea?
5 If there was only a little clean water who should have it first: farmers, factories, families, fish? Give your reasons.

E A water quiz
1 What is water made of?
2 How much of your body is water?
3 How much water is used to make a) a ton of cement b) a ton of paper c) a gallon of beer? (i) 60,000 (ii) 800 (iii) 350 gallons.

(Answers: see page 61)

9 The boy who cried wolf

Once upon a time there was a very naughty shepherd-boy. He often fell asleep while he was watching his sheep. And he told lies. The villagers shook their heads and said, 'That boy will come to a bad end.'

One day, when he was feeling very bored, the boy decided to play a practical joke on the villagers. He ran down the hill.
'Wolf, wolf!' he cried. 'Help, come quickly. Wolf!'
All the villagers seized their spears and ran to help him. But there was no wolf.
'He heard you,' the naughty boy lied, 'and ran away.'
When everyone had gone, he started to laugh.

Three weeks later, when he was feeling very bored indeed, he decided to play the same trick again.
'Wolf, wolf!' he shouted. 'Help, come quickly. Wolf!'
Most of the villagers hurried to help him. This time the boy laughed at them.
'Ha, ha. There wasn't a wolf,' he said. 'What a good joke!'
The villagers were very angry.
'Lies are not jokes,' they said.

Two days later the boy woke up suddenly. He had fallen asleep in the afternoon sun. What was that big dark animal coming towards his flock? Suddenly it seized a lamb.
'Wolf!' screamed the boy. 'Wolf. Help, come quickly. Wolf!'
But none of the villagers came to help him. He screamed again. The wolf heard him and licked its lips.
'I like lamb,' it thought, 'but shepherd-boy tastes much nicer.'

When the shepherd-boy didn't come home that night, some of the villagers went to look for him. They found a few bones.

The End

The boy who cried wolf

Presentation 1

9

A Comprehension
1 Was the boy in the story good at his job? Why/why not?
2 What did the villagers say?
3 Describe the practical joke the boy played one day. What happened? Why did he do it?
4 Why do you think all the villagers came to help him the first time?
5 Did they all come the second time?
6 Why didn't anyone come when the boy told the truth?
7 What happened to the boy?
8 What do you think the villagers said when they found his bones?
9 Did the story frighten you?
10 Would it frighten a young child?

B Should we tell stories like this to young children?

a State the case FOR
1 It's wrong to fall asleep at work, to play tricks, to tell lies. Children must learn this.
2 The fable has a moral. Shepherd-boy tells lies; lazy; wastes villagers' time. Wolf punishes him.
3 Children like stories—listen. Don't really believe in the wolf—learn the lesson.
   Every country has fables.

b State the case AGAINST
1 It's wrong to frighten children—hear the story—can't sleep. Dream of hungry wolves.
2 The punishment is too severe. Some children believe the story—learn to tell the truth, but for the wrong reason—fear.
3 Other children laugh at the story—think the boy's death a joke. Too much cruelty in the world—keep it out of children's stories.

C What's your opinion?
1 Which moral fits the story best? Give reasons for your decision.
   a It's dangerous to fall asleep at work.
   b If you play tricks on older people they won't help you later.
   c If you tell too many lies, people won't ever believe you.
2 How do *you* think we should teach young children to tell the truth?
   a Punish them severely when they tell lies.
   b Tell them stories with a moral: e.g. The boy who cried wolf.
   c Teach them rules: e.g. Do not tell lies.
   d Set a good example: i.e. Always tell the truth ourselves.

D Talking points
1 Can you tell a children's story that everyone likes? Is there any cruelty in it? Does cruelty matter in children's stories/films/T.V. programmes?
2 What frightened you when you were young? Tell us about it.
3 Have you ever played a practical joke? Who laughed?

E Fire Alarm.
If someone suddenly screamed 'Fire!' what would you do?

10 Beauty *and* brains

This story is taken from The Use of Lateral Thinking by Edward de Bono. First published by Jonathan Cape (1967). Published by Penguin (1971).
©Copyright Edward de Bono.

Beauty and brains

Presentation 1 **10**

A Comprehension
1 What was Marco's problem?
2 What did Pedro agree to do?
3 Why didn't Bella want to marry Pedro?
4 What did Pedro offer Marco and Bella?
5 What did Bella have to do? Explain.
6 What did Pedro put in the bag?
7 Who saw him?
8 What did Pedro expect to happen?
9 What would have happened if Bella had complained?
10 What would have happened if she had refused to take a pebble?
11 When Bella took the pebble, what did she do?
12 Do you think it was an accident?
13 What did Bella tell Pedro to do?
14 What colour was the pebble in the bag?
15 What did this mean?
16 Why couldn't Pedro complain?
17 What do you think happened next?

B Retell the story
a Give Bella's point of view—begin: 'Pedro tried to trick me...
b Give Pedro's point of view—begin: 'I wanted to help Bella...
c Whose side are *you* on? Why?
d How would Marco tell the story?

C Do you agree or disagree with the following statements? Give your reasons.
1 Pedro was a wicked man: he used to send people to prison.
2 Pedro was a kind man: he wanted to help Marco and Bella.
3 Pedro was a lonely old man: he wanted to marry Bella very much.
4 Marco was a weak person: he shouldn't have got into debt.
5 Marco was a good father: he didn't want his daughter to starve.
6 Bella was very clever: she found the answer to a very difficult problem.
7 Bella was dishonest: she tricked Pedro.
8 Bella was foolish: sensible girls marry rich men.
9 Women should marry for love, not money.
10 Fathers have a right to choose their daughters' husbands.
11 If someone tricks you, it's all right to trick them.
12 The end justifies the means.

D Talking points
1 What kind of person would you like to marry? Describe your ideal partner.
2 Why do people sometimes need to borrow money? What kind of things do they want to buy?
3 If *you* needed to borrow some money what would you do?
4 Have you ever had to make a difficult decision? What was the problem? What did you do?
5 Can you tell a story in which someone plays a clever trick?

E Two proverbs
Neither a borrower nor a lender be.
True love finds a way.

11 TOO OLD AT TWENTY

DO YOU REMEMBER SALLY GREEN?

Do you remember Sally Green, the swimming star? She was the girl who broke all the records at the last Olympics. Where is she now? Last week our reporter, Tom Parker, went to see Sally in her Californian home.

Tom Is it true that you don't swim at all now?

Sally I'm afraid so. I'm too old.

Tom But you're only twenty!

Sally That's too old for a swimmer. If I swam in an international competition now, I wouldn't win. So I'd rather not swim at all.

Tom But don't you enjoy swimming?

Sally I used to, when I was small. But if you enter for big competitions you have to work very hard. I used to get up at 6 a.m. to go to the pool. I had to train before school, after school and at weekends. I swam 35 miles every week!

Tom But you were famous at fifteen. And look at all those cups.

Sally Would *you* like to polish them?

It's true that I have some wonderful memories. I enjoyed visiting other countries, and the Olympics were very exciting. But I missed more important things. While other girls were growing up, I was swimming. What can I do now?

SALLY WINS AGAIN!

Too old at twenty

Presentation 1 **11**

A Comprehension
1 What is Tom Parker's job?
2 Why was Sally famous at fifteen?
3 Which country does she live in?
4 Why doesn't she swim any more?
5 What did she dislike about her life as an international swimmer?
6 Why is the reporter surprised?
7 What does Sally think of her cups?
8 What are her good memories?
9 Can you suggest what 'I missed more important things' means?
10 Has she any ideas about her future?

B What's life like for a swimming star?

a State the ADVANTAGES.
1 Famous at an early age—everyone knows you; people want to meet you. Reporters interview you; photo in papers, magazines etc.
2 Exciting life—visit other countries for competitions. Swim in big races—break records.
3 Rewards—prizes, cups etc. Wonderful memories.

b State the DISADVANTAGES.
1 Famous too young—no private life; miss the things other girls do. Reporters ask silly questions. Can only win races when young.
2 Hard life—have to get up early; train for hours; swim miles etc. Don't enjoy the sport any more. Travel abroad—don't see much.
3 Can't live on memories—no future.

C What's your opinion?
1 Is it more important to enjoy swimming or to win races?
2 Do you think Sally was right to give up swimming? Why/why not?
3 How would you describe a 'normal' life for a girl of fifteen?
4 Do you think it's a good idea to visit other countries when you're young? Why/why not? Would *you* like to travel?
5 What advice would you give Sally? When will *you* be too old to enjoy life?

D Talking points
1 What can you tell us about the Olympic Games? When did they first start? Where are they held? Name some of the events. Who hold the records?
2 Why do people try to break records? What's the point of swimming faster or running faster than everyone else?
3 Why do swimmers, athletes etc. have to train so hard?
4 Talk about the famous athletes, swimmers and sportsmen in our country.
5 Here are some famous names: Mozart, Picasso, Shakespeare, Julius Caesar, Nobel. When did these men live? What nationality were they? What did they do?
6 Do people always have to work hard to be famous? Why/why not?
7 Are young people often famous? Why/why not?
8 Why have there been more famous men than women? Can you name a famous woman? What is/was she famous for?

E Suggested Reading:
Books in the series: *'Lives of Achievement'* General Editor ME Carter MBEBA (Longman)

12 A good alibi?

Inspector Sharp Good afternoon, Biggs. Have you any news on that robbery in Camford?
  Constable Biggs Yes, sir. I got a statement from Bates, but he's got a good alibi. Here it is.

> ### Statement
> On Wednesday, March 8th, 1972, I, John Arthur Bates, went to see my sister, Mrs Elizabeth Brown. It was her birthday. She lives in Newton. I left my home in London soon after 9 a.m. The milkman saw me. My car is a red mini, no. XYZ 259 K. I drove along the A8. I filled up with petrol near Shepherds Green and had some coffee at the Cosy Cafe in Burton. The waiter told me there had been an accident near Brent:- two pilots were driving to London from the airport and had hit a lorry. The road was still blocked. So I took the A246 to Maresby, and then the A247 to Newton. I stopped in High Wick and went to the market. I bought some flowers for my sister. I reached Newton in time for lunch at 1 o'clock.

Constable Biggs I've checked his alibi with the milkman, the man at the garage, and the waiter in the café. There *was* an accident on the A 8 and the flowers are still in his sister's house.
Inspector Sharp Hm. Bring me the Drivers' Guide. Look up High Wick, and then look at the map. He *could* have gone to Camford.

Drivers' Guide
High Wick: 9,945   Map 19.
London 44,   Burton 12,
Newton 15,   Maresby 14.
Market day   Tue/Sat.
early closing   Thurs.

A good alibi?   Presentation 2 12

A What had happened?
1. Had there been a robbery or a murder in Camford?
2. Which policemen were dealing with the case?
3. What had Biggs got from Bates?
4. What did Biggs think of Bates' alibi?
5. Had Biggs checked the alibi?
6. What did Inspector Sharp think?

B Check Bates' alibi.
Look at his statement, the map, and the Drivers' Guide.
1. Where is Bates' home?
2. Why did he go to see his sister?
3. What day of the week was it?
4. Who saw him leave?
5. What kind of car has he got?
6. Which road did he take first?
7. How far is it from London to Newton?
8. What was Bates' average speed?
9. How many times did he stop? What did he do? Who did he speak to?
10. Why didn't he go through Brent?
11. Where did he buy some flowers?
12. How did Biggs check Bates' alibi?
13. Did he leave anything out?
14. Which road goes direct to Newton?
15. Could Bates have taken the A 7 from *London*? Why/why not?
16. Which road is Camford on?
17. How could you get from Burton to Camford?
18. Can Bates prove he went to Maresby?
19. Where did he say he'd stopped between Burton and Newton?
20. When is market day in High Wick?

C Would you be a good detective?
1. What do you think of Bates' alibi?
2. What further questions would you ask Bates?
3. Which towns would you visit?
4. Which shops would you go to?
5. Who would you interview?
6. What questions would you ask?
7. How could you find out if Bates had taken the A 247 or not?
8. How would you find other suspects?

D Talking points
1. Is it easy to remember exactly what you did on a certain day? What did *you* do three weeks ago today? Could you state every detail?
2. What are the most common crimes in your country? Is it easy to catch the criminals? Why/why not?
3. Would you like to be a detective? Why/why not? What else do policemen do?

E Play a game: Alibi.
1. Suggest a crime: e.g. Someone stole a car at lunchtime on Monday.
2. Choose two 'suspects'. Send them outside the class to make up an alibi.
3. Prepare some questions to ask the suspects: e.g. 'What were you doing at lunchtime last Monday? What did you eat?'
4. Call in one suspect and interview him. Then call in the other and ask him the same questions. If they both give the same answers they are innocent; if they give different answers they are guilty.

13 *Music or* MONEY?

1. *Mr Davies (quietly)* Why aren't you doing your homework?
   Martin I'll do it later, Dad. I must get these chords right first. Our group's playing in a concert on Saturday.

2. *Mr Davies (laughs)* Oh, is it? You'll be making records next, will you?
   Martin We hope so. The man from 'Dream Discs' is coming to the concert. So I'd better play well.

3. *Mr Davies* You'd better get on with your homework! You can practise all day Saturday.
   Martin Oh Dad. You don't understand at all. This concert could change my life.

4. *Mr Davies* It certainly could! You've got exams next month. Important ones. If you don't get a good certificate, you won't get a decent job.
   Martin (rudely) I don't need a certificate to play the guitar. And I don't want a boring old job in a bank either.

5. *Mr Davies (angrily)* Oh don't you? Whose boring old job paid for this house? *And* for that guitar?
   Martin (sighs) Yours, I know. But *I'd* rather be happy than rich.

Music or money?   Presentation 1 13

A Comprehension
1 What was Martin doing when his father came in?
2 Why wasn't he doing his homework?
3 Was Mr Davies pleased or annoyed?
4 Why did Martin think the concert on Saturday was important?
5 Why did his father disagree?
6 Where does Mr Davies work?
7 Why doesn't Martin want to work in a bank?
8 What made Mr Davies angry?
9 Why do you think Martin was rude?

B Report the arguments.
a What did Mr Davies tell his wife?
1 Worried about Martin—playing the guitar, not doing homework. Dreaming of concerts, records.
2 Exams next month—if he fails, no certificate; won't get a job.
3 Doesn't understand that a good job is important—good pay, security.
4 Rude to me—my job boring. Ungrateful—house, guitar. Stupid—doesn't want to be rich.

b What did Martin tell his friends?
1 Dad angry with me—practising the guitar, not doing homework.
2 Concert on Saturday—man from 'Dream Discs'—change my life. Dad talks of homework, exams, jobs.
3 Want to be a musician—not a bank clerk; interesting, exciting life. Guitarists don't need certificates.
4 Dad doesn't understand—talks of money, security; I'd rather be happy.

C Would you like to work in a bank?
1 Are you good at arithmetic?
2 Are you careful in all your work?
3 Would you like a secure life?
4 Are you willing to take more exams?
5 Would you like a five-day week?

Would you like to be a musician?
1 Can you play an instrument well?
2 Would you like to work at weekends?
3 Would you like a risky life?
4 Do you like travelling?
5 Can you eat meals at odd times?

If you answer 'Yes' to Q. 1 and at least 2 more questions you'd like the life. Who do you agree with, Martin or his father? Give your reasons.

D Talking points
1 What are your views on homework? Does it interfere with your hobbies?
2 Can you play a musical instrument? Do you practise enough? Why/why not?
3 Who is your favourite musician? What is your favourite record? Why?
4 Are there any secure jobs for musicians? If so, what?
5 Suggest some jobs for which you need certificates. Are they the best jobs?
6 Why do fathers often want their sons to do the same jobs as they did?
7 What do most mothers hope their daughters will do? Why?
8 Would you rather have a secure job or a risky one? Give your reasons.
9 Is it easy for parents and children to understand each other? Why/why not?

E Find out how much the following people earn: a bank clerk, a bank manager, a famous pop-star, an ordinary band-player.

14 Too much _ _ _
too little ...

a Too much

b Too little

Too much...too little...
Presentation 2 **14**

A Look at the photos
a Too much...
1. Is the boy fat or thin?
2. Has he got anything in his mouth?
3. What do you think it is?
4. How old do you think he is?
5. What's he doing?
6. Does he look happy or sad?
7. Is he from a poor country or a rich one? How can you tell?
8. Do you think he gets too much to eat? Why/why not?

b Too little...
1. Does the child look healthy or ill?
2. When do you think she last had a meal?
3. Do you think she ever gets enough to eat?
4. She's from a poor family, isn't she?
5. Is she from a rich country?
6. Why isn't she playing?
7. Do you think she will live to grow up? Why/why not?

B Children today have too much to eat
a State the argument.
1. Too many fat children—eat too much; large meals; sweets, biscuits, chocolate between meals.
2. Fat people—unhealthy; have more diseases, die young.
3. Children should have a sensible diet—eat to live, not live to eat.

b State the counter-argument.
1. Many children are starving—too little food; droughts, famines in some countries.
2. Many children are ill—don't get the right food.
3. Children in poor countries are dying—rich countries should help.

C What's your opinion?
1. Do you think children today get too much to eat? Do *you*?
2. Do you think sweets are bad for you? How many do you eat every week?
3. Would you rather be fat or thin? Give your reasons.
4. How can starving children best be helped? Should rich countries/people give food to poor countries/people? Why/why not?
5. Choose sensible meals for a day from the following list of food: milk meat cake bread cheese fish chocolate eggs rice oranges beans ice-cream potatoes cabbage coffee tea butter.

D Talking points
1. Describe the best meal you've ever had.
2. Has there ever been a bad drought in our country? If so, tell us what happened.
3. Have you seen pictures of starving children? If so, where? What country were they from? Was there a famine?
4. Do you know where *your* food comes from? If so, tell us.

E A saying
Enough is as good as a feast.

15 Find the right job

Peter Dent

Abilities	Good at woodwork, games. Bad at maths, English.
Interests	Cars, football.
Character	Helpful, friendly.

Mary West

Abilities	Good at English, history. Bad at chemistry.
Interests	Listening to music, reading.
Character	Quiet, shy.

Wheel of jobs:
- builder, dress-maker — work at making things
- astronomer, chemist — work in science
- farmer, sailor — work out doors
- author, librarian — work with words
- doctor, teacher — work with people
- actor, musician — work in the arts
- typist, solicitor — work in an office
- banker, accountant — work with figures

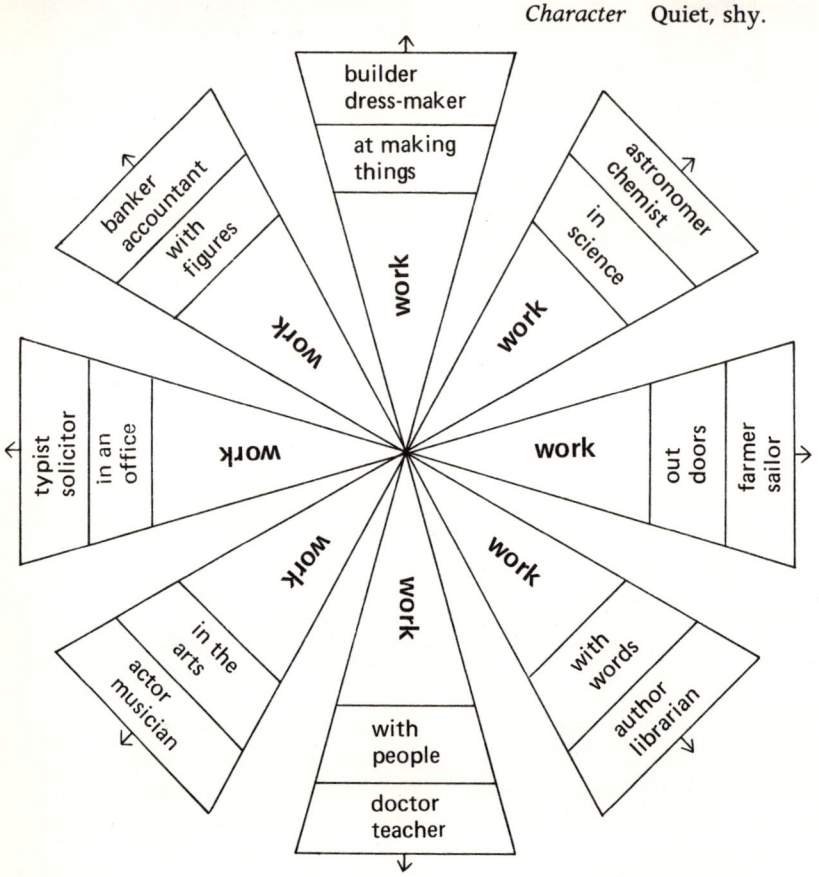

Anne Short

Abilities	Good at needlework, art. Bad at games (weak back)
Interests	Fond of children and animals.
Character	Lively, kind.

Paul Hart

Abilities	Good at maths, physics. Bad at art.
Interests	Stamps, 'Space'.
Character	Careful, hard-working.

Find the right job

Presentation 2 **15**

A Comprehension

a Look at the notes on the children
1. What is Peter good at/bad at?
2. What are his interests?
3. What's his character like?
4. What abilities has Anne got?
5. Why is she bad at games?
6. What is she interested in?
7. What sort of person is she?
8. How do Mary's abilities and interests differ from Anne's?
9. Are they the same sort of person?
10. Compare Paul with Peter.

b Look at the diagram
1. How many groups is work divided into? What are they?
2. How many examples of jobs are given?
3. Whose jobs are with words?
4. Who works outdoors?
5. Where do typists work?
6. What do bankers work with?
7. Does an astronomer work in science or in the arts?
8. What kind of work does a builder do?
9. Which jobs are with people?

B Find the right jobs for the children.
Use the notes below.

Name a Which jobs could they do?
1. Peter: could be a builder—good at woodwork, helpful.
2. Anne: could be a dressmaker—good at needlework, art.
3. Mary: could be a librarian—likes books, good with words.
4. Paul: could be an astronomer—interested in 'Space'; good at physics, maths.

b Which jobs shouldn't they do?
Shouldn't be an accountant—bad at maths.
Shouldn't be a nurse—weak back.
Shouldn't be a teacher—quiet, shy.
Shouldn't be a doctor—seems more interested in things than in people.

C What's your opinion?
1. Do you agree with the suggestions in B? Why/why not?
2. What other jobs would you suggest for the children? Give reasons.
3. Are there any other jobs they should *not* choose? If so, which and why?
4. Do you agree with the way the jobs are grouped? Why/why not?
5. What are *your* abilities and interests? Which jobs could you do?
6. How would you describe your character? Which jobs shouldn't you do?
7. Which jobs would you suggest for yourself/your friends? Give reasons.
8. Would you want the same job all your life? Why/why not?

D Talking points
1. Could you describe a day in the life of a teacher/doctor/builder?
2. How can school children find out about different jobs?
3. Who's the best person to advise you when you're choosing a job?
4. Can people change their abilities? If so, how? What about character?

E A piece of advice.
Find the right job—don't be a square peg in a round hole.

16 *Books belong to the Past*

Readers' letters

Sir,
I visited my old school yesterday. It hasn't changed in thirty years. The pupils were sitting in the same desks and reading the same books. When are schools going to move into the modern world? Books belong to the past. In our homes radio and television bring us knowledge of the world. We can see and hear the truth for ourselves. If we want entertainment most of us prefer a modern film to a classical novel. In the business world computers store information, so that we no longer need encyclopaedias and dictionaries. But in the schools teachers and pupils still use books. There should be a radio and television set in every classroom, and a library of tapes and records in every school. The children of today will rarely open a book when they leave school. The children of tomorrow won't need to read and write at all.

M.P. Miller
London

Books belong to the past

Presentation 1 **16**

A Comprehension
1 Where had Mr Miller been?
2 Why wasn't he pleased?
3 How old do you think he is? Why?
4 How do people get information and entertainment in the modern world?
5 What does Mr Miller think schools should use instead of books?
6 What does he say about the future?
7 Do you agree with him? Why/why not?
8 How would you reply to his letter?

B Do books belong to the past?
a State Mr Miller's argument.
1 Schools use books—should move into modern world; books past.
2 Homes: radio, T.V. for knowledge of world—see, hear truth.
  Entertainment: films, not novels.
  Business: computers, information—don't need dictionaries etc.
3 Classrooms should have radio, T.V. Schools: library of tapes etc.
4 Today: children won't *want* to read when they leave school.
  Tomorrow: no *need* to read.

b State the counter-argument.
1 Schools *are* in the modern world—books belong to present, future. Radio, T.V. etc. can help teachers, but still need books.
2 Homes: newspapers, magazines—radio, T.V. not always right.
  Entertainment: many people like novels; films have scripts.
  Business: computers expensive.
3 Today: more people *want* to read—more books sold; more *need* to read—notices, forms, letters.

C A Reading Questionnaire
1 How many books do you use in this class? Which subject uses the most books? Did your parents use the same books when they were at school?
2 What was the title of the last book you *chose* to read? Was it fiction or non-fiction? What's the best book you've ever read? Why did you enjoy it?
3 What sort of fiction do you prefer: novels, adventure stories, tales of the past? Do you read poetry?
4 When did you last use a dictionary/ encyclopaedia? How often do you use reference books?
5 Which of the following do you read regularly: newspapers, magazines, comics?
6 Do you think you'll 'rarely open a book' when you leave school? Why/why not?
7 Can you remember everything you read yesterday? Was it just books? What do you think you'll have to read in adult life?

D Talking points
1 What were your parents' schools like? Do they think schools have changed?
2 Do you think schools will be the same in thirty years' time? Why/why not?
3 In which subjects would radio/T.V./tape-recorders be most helpful? Why?
4 Can people who can't read and write get good jobs? Why/why not?

E Play a game: Spaceship.
Imagine you are packing for a long voyage into space. You may take three books with you. Which would you choose and why?

17 Focus on success

What makes a man successful? The experts have an answer. He must grow up in a good home. The seeds of success are sown in childhood. Some children are unlucky. They grow up in poor homes. Their fathers can't get jobs, so their families never have any money. They live in small, dirty houses, and don't get enough to eat. Their parents are often ill and sometimes die. They can't afford to go to school, so they don't get any education. They haven't got a chance.

Let's look at an example:

Date of birth	12.2.1809
Place of birth	U.S.A.
Father	Farm-worker. Moved frequently.
Mother	Died when he was nine. Brought up by step-mother.
Home	One-room cabin. Floor made of dirt. Bed covered with skins.
Education	One year at school.
1828	Went to Illinois alone. Took various jobs: (i) store-keeper (ii) labourer (iii) postmaster Borrowed books and read all night. Taught himself law.
1834	Elected to the State of Illinois Legislature.
1847	Seat in U.S. Congress.
1861–1865	President of the U.S.A.
Died	15.4.1865

According to the experts Abraham Lincoln didn't have a chance. What made *him* successful? Could the experts be wrong?

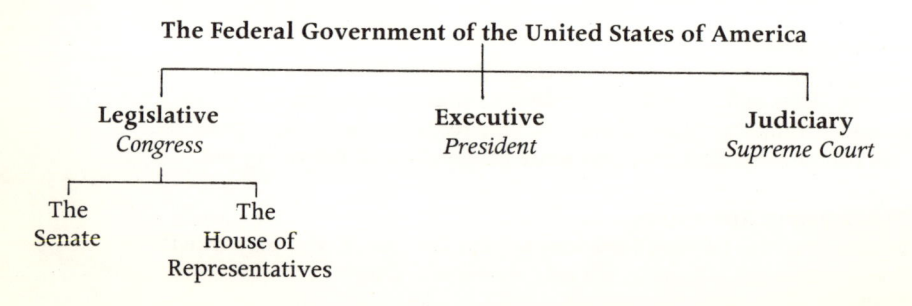

The Federal Government of the United States of America

Legislative	Executive	Judiciary
Congress	*President*	*Supreme Court*

Congress:
- The Senate
- The House of Representatives

Focus on success

Presentation 2 **17**

A Comprehension
1 Are some people more successful than others?
2 Why? What do the experts say?
3 Why are some children unlucky?

Abraham Lincoln's childhood
1 Where was he born? How long ago?
2 What did his father do?
3 What happened to his mother?
4 Who brought him up afterwards?
5 What was his home like?
6 How much education did he get?
7 Do you think he had a good start in life?
8 Do you think he liked being poor?

4 What do the experts mean by a poor home?
5 Does the writer agree with them? Let's look at his example:

Abraham Lincoln as an adult
1 Where did he go in 1828?
2 What jobs did he get? Were they good ones?
3 How did he spend his free time?
4 Who taught him law?
5 Describe his political career: what happened in 1834, 1847, 1861?
6 Would you say he was successful?
7 What made him successful?

B What makes a person successful?
a *Summarise the experts' argument.*
1 Seeds of success—childhood. Successful people—good homes.
2 Some children—poor homes:— fathers—no jobs, money; one or both parents ill, or die.
3 Houses—small, dirty. Food—poor, not enough.
4 No school, no education— haven't got a chance.

b *Summarise a counter-argument.*
1 Many successful people—'poor' homes. Want to escape poverty etc.
2 Work hard; teach themselves. Parents—no money, but kind, honest; help children—love them.
3 Rich parents—lazy, spoilt children; don't work, fail.
4 Experts only notice money etc.—ignore ability, desire to succeed.

C What's your opinion?
1 Do you agree with the experts or the writer? What's wrong/right with their arguments?
2 Do you think Abraham Lincoln is typical of people from 'poor' homes, or was he an exception?
3 Are all children of rich parents spoilt and lazy? Give examples.
4 What's the most important thing parents can give their children?
5 What does the writer mean by success? What do *you* think it is?

D Talking points
1 Describe your idea of a good home and a happy childhood.
2 What is meant by success in school life? Do you know of anyone who failed at school but became successful later? What problems can success bring?

E A motto:
'If at first you don't succeed, try, try again.'

18

FORUM

Should school children take part-time jobs?

Editor This month our panel looks at part-time jobs. Are they good for school children or not?

Headmaster Definitely not. Children have got two full-time jobs already: growing up and going to school. Part-time jobs make them so tired they fall asleep in class.

Mrs Barnes I agree. I know school hours are short, but there's homework as well. And children need a lot of sleep.

Mr Barnes Young children perhaps, but some boys stay at school until they're eighteen or nineteen. A part-time job can't harm them. In fact, it's good for them. They earn their pocket-money instead of asking their parents for it. And they see something of the world outside school.

Businessman You're absolutely right. Boys learn a lot from a part-time job. And we mustn't forget that some families need the extra money. If the pupils didn't take part-time jobs they couldn't stay at school.

Editor Well, we seem to be equally divided: two for, and two against. What do our readers think?

Headmaster

Businessman

Mr Barnes

Mrs Barnes

Should school children take part-time jobs?

Presentation 1

18

A Comprehension
1 Who are the members of the panel?
2 Why do you think they were chosen?
3 What are they discussing?
4 Why does the headmaster think part-time jobs are bad? Who agrees?
5 What point does she add?
6 Does her husband agree with her?
7 What's his opinion about part-time jobs for older pupils?
8 Does the businessman agree with Mr Barnes or with the headmaster?
9 In what ways does he think part-time jobs are useful?
10 How does the panel divide?

B Should school children take part-time jobs?

a State the case FOR
1 Good for older boys—earn pocket-money, don't ask parents.
2 See world, learn a lot.
3 Help their families—extra money. Help themselves—can afford to stay at school.

b State the case AGAINST
1 Bad for children—two jobs already: growing up, going to school.
2 Children—a lot of sleep; part-time jobs—tired, sleep in class.
3 School hours short, but homework. Education important, not money.

C What do you think?
1 Is growing up a job? Why/why not? What about going to school?
2 Do children need a lot of sleep? Why *do* some pupils fall asleep in class?
3 Is it better to earn pocket-money or to be given it? Why?
4 What can you learn from a job that you can't learn at school?
5 The speakers only mention boys. Should girls do part-time jobs? Why/why not?
6 Part-time jobs can be done at different times:—before school/after school/at weekends/in the holidays. What are the advantages and disadvantages of these times?
7 Here are some part-time jobs:—cleaning cars/helping in a shop/looking after children/helping in the garden. If you wanted a part-time job which would you choose and why?

D Talking points
1 Have you ever fallen asleep in class? What happened?
2 What are the advantages and disadvantages of staying at school until you are eighteen or nineteen?
3 In most countries it is more common for students at college or university to take part-time jobs than school children. Can you suggest why?

E A problem:
Mario is sixteen and very clever. His teacher thinks he can win a scholarship to university. BUT his father is ill and there are three younger children. If Mario left school he could get a job and help his family. Should he leave school or not? What do *you* think?

Viewpoint

More people live to 80

WHAT'S WRONG WITH TODAY'S YOUTH

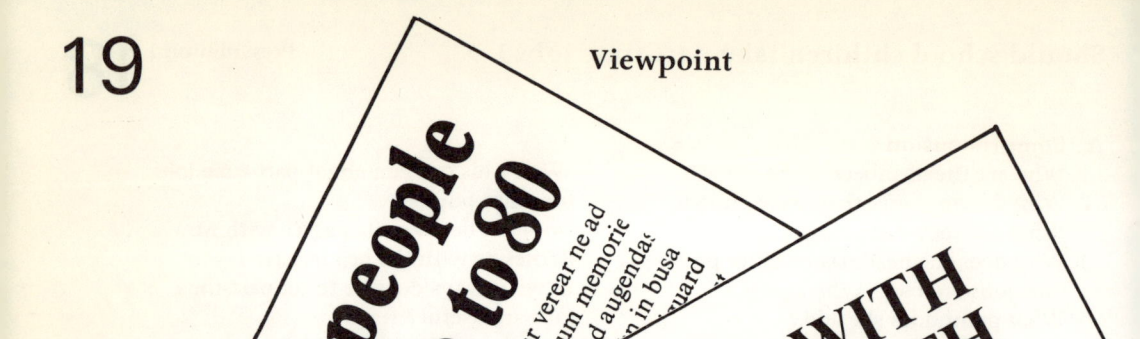

Why can't I do what I like?

asks Helen Smith   aged 16

I hope I never grow old! My grandfather lives with us and he's making my life a misery. When I was small he was kind and cheerful. But now he's always complaining and criticising. I mustn't interrupt when he's talking. It's rude. He doesn't like my clothes. 'Nice girls don't dress like that.' I shouldn't wear make-up. 'Natural beauty is best.' Sometimes he interferes with my homework.

'When I was young we used to do maths differently,' he says. Honestly, he's so old he doesn't know anything. But that doesn't stop him criticising me. He doesn't like my friends or my favourite records. 'You're making too much noise,' he calls. 'I can't get to sleep.' When he's not complaining he's asking questions. 'Where are you going? Where have you been? Why aren't you helping your mother?' He thinks I'm six, not sixteen. Anyway, why can't I do what I like? It's my life, not his.

Why can't I do what I like?

Presentation 1 — 19

A Comprehension
1. How old is Helen Smith?
2. Why doesn't she want to grow old?
3. How has her grandfather changed since she was small?
4. Why does he think she's rude?
5. Why doesn't he like her clothes?
6. What are his views on make-up?
7. Why can't he do her maths?
8. Why does Helen think he shouldn't criticise her?
9. Why doesn't he like her friends?
10. What keeps him awake at night?
11. What questions does he ask Helen?
12. Why does this make her angry?
13. Do you think Helen makes her grandfather happy? Why/why not?

B Two points of view
a State Helen's point of view.
1. Hope never grow old—grandfather making life a misery.
   Small—kind and cheerful.
   Now—complaining, criticising.
2. Mustn't interrupt—rude.
   Doesn't like clothes, make-up.
3. Interferes with homework—maths different; so old he knows nothing—criticises me.
4. Dislikes friends, records—too much noise, can't sleep.
5. Asking questions—*my* life.

b State her grandfather's viewpoint.
1. Old—live with my son and family.
   Helen—used to be quiet, polite.
   Now doesn't listen, interrupts.
2. Wears terrible clothes, too much make-up—not nice, natural.
3. Try to help with homework—maths difficult now.
4. Try to like her friends, records—noise till midnight, can't sleep.
5. Worries her mother—doesn't help; goes out, doesn't say where.
   Rude, noisy and selfish girl.

C What's your opinion?
1. How could Helen and her grandfather be happier? What would you suggest?
2. Why do old people have different views about clothes, make-up etc. from teenagers? Who's right?
3. Are *you* looking forward to growing old? Why/why not?
4. Are the following statements true or false? Give your reasons.
   - i Old people don't know anything.
   - ii Life is easier for old people than it used to be.
   - iii Grandparents spoil their grandchildren.
   - iv Three generations can't live in the same house.

D Talking points
1. In some countries old people live alone, or in hospitals. Do you think this is right? Why/why not? What's the best way to look after old people?
2. Is it fair to keep other people awake? What happens in your family?
3. What would happen if everybody did what they liked?

E Find out how your grandparents lived when they were teenagers.

20 FORGET IT?

Continuing our story of Mary and Kate at school. It's Saturday and Mary has gone to watch her friend Paul play in a football match.

Panel 1: YOU PLAYED MARVELLOUSLY, PAUL. / I KNEW YOU WERE WATCHING. COME ON. I'LL HAVE A QUICK SHOWER, AND THEN WE'LL GO. MEET ME BY THE CLOAKROOM DOOR IN TEN MINUTES.

Panel 2: THAT'S NOT YOUR COAT, IS IT? / SSH. COME ON.

Panel 3: WHAT DID YOU PUT IN YOUR POCKET? / NOTHING. DON'T ASK QUESTIONS. / BUT... / LOOK, FORGET IT OR I'LL FIND ANOTHER GIRLFRIEND.

Panel 4: LATER... THANK YOU FOR A VERY NICE TEA, MRS. COBB. / COME AGAIN, PAUL. / WHAT A NICE BOY!

Panel 5: £5 WAS STOLEN FROM J. BROOKS COAT POCKET LAST SATURDAY AFTERNOON. ANYONE WHO KNOWS ANYTHING ABOUT IT SHOULD GO TO THE HEADMASTER'S OFFICE. / LOOK AT THAT!

Panel 6: HOW HORRIBLE. WHO DID IT, DO YOU THINK? / I'VE HEARD THAT PEOPLE SUSPECT BARKER.

Panel 7: THAT UGLY LITTLE BOY IN THE SECOND YEAR? / YES. WELL HE HASN'T GOT ANY FRIENDS. PERHAPS HE WANTED SOME MONEY INSTEAD.

Panel 8: BARKER'S A THIEF, A THIEF. / I'M NOT, I'M NOT. / HEADMA[STER'S] OFFICE ←

Forget it?

Presentation 1 **20**

A Comprehension
1 When was the football match?
2 Why did Mary go to watch?
3 Describe Paul. How did he play?
4 When and where did he arrange to meet Mary?
5 What did Mary see when she arrived?
6 What did she ask Paul?
7 What did Paul reply?
8 Why did Mary stop asking questions?
9 Where did Paul and Mary have tea?
10 What did Mrs Cobb think of Paul?
11 What did Kate show Mary on Monday?
12 Who was suspected? Describe him.
13 Why did Kate think he might be the thief?
14 Why was Mary worried?

B Should Mary go to the Headmaster?
a State the reasons FOR
1 Met Paul after match—hand on wrong coat; put something in pocket. Wouldn't answer her. Cross—forget it.
2 Could have been Brooks' coat; could have put £5 in pocket. Behaved in a guilty way.
3 People suspect Barker—not popular; calling him a thief. Crying—says he's not.
4 Barker could be innocent— Paul could be guilty. Mary knows *something*.

b State the reasons AGAINST
1 Paul—nice boy, popular etc. Mary lucky—his girl-friend; doesn't want to lose him.
2 Paul—mistake over coat. Mary—didn't *see* any money. Stupid to ask questions after a match—players tired.
3 Barker could be a thief—no friends— wants money. Crying—frightened, guilty.
4 Wrong to tell tales; get your friends into trouble. Mary doesn't *know* anything.

C What's your opinion?
1 Should Mary go to the Headmaster or not? What else could she do?
2 Who could Mary ask for advice? Should she talk to Kate or not?
3 Do you think she should talk to Paul about the notice? Why/why not?
4 Why does Mary's mother think Paul is a nice boy? Do you think he is?
5 Why is Paul more popular than Barker? Do you think Barker has a girl-friend?
6 How do you think Barker felt when he was called a thief?
7 What do you think the Headmaster will do if no one goes to his office?

D Talking points
1 What gets stolen in schools? Is it easy to find the thief?
2 What do people steal outside schools? Why? How can they be stopped?
3 Can you explain why some people are more popular than others?
4 How should friends behave towards each other? What is a true friend?

E Suggested reading:
'Oliver Twist' by Charles Dickens. New Method Supplementary Reader Stage 4 (Longman)

21 Who makes the decisions?

```
              Huntingford High School
                  School Council
A meeting of the School Council will be held in the
Dining Hall on Wednesday, 21st June 1972, at 4.00 pm.
                      Agenda
1 Minutes of the meeting held on 18th May 1972, and
  matters arising.
2 Report of the Entertainments Sub-Committee.
3 School uniform: 4th year proposal to abolish uniform.
4 Any other business.

        Signed: J. Winters (VI Science)
                Secretary
```

25 Station Road,
Huntingford,
Hunts,
England.

20th June, 1972.

Dear Maria,
    I'm sorry I haven't written for so long. It's been a very busy term, and we've just had exams. I hope I've passed. Tomorrow we've got a School Council Meeting. I'm one of the representatives for the Fourth Year, and I'm going to speak about school uniform. We want to abolish it. It's so ugly and expensive. You don't wear uniform in Italy, do you? Do you have a School Council? There are more staff than pupils in ours. If we can't agree on a proposal we take a vote. Guess who wins! Well, I must prepare my speech. I promise I'll write you a <u>long</u> letter during the holidays.

        Love from,
           Carol

P.S. Here's the agenda for the meeting. I thought you might like to see it.

Who makes the decisions?

Presentation 2

21

A Comprehension
1 Why hasn't Carol written to Maria for so long? Who *is* Maria?
2 What does Carol tell her about?
3 What questions does she ask her?
4 When and where will the School Council meeting be held?
5 What's on the agenda?
6 Which year is the secretary in?

B DEBATE School uniform should be abolished.
a Make Carol's speech, using the notes below. Begin as follows:
'Mr Chairman, on behalf of the 4th year, I wish to propose the motion that school uniform should be abolished...
1 School uniform—ugly, old-fashioned. Makes pretty girls plain, ugly girls uglier. Same for boys.
2 Important to learn to dress well—for jobs, social life. Pupils don't like uniform—don't look after it; dirty, untidy.
3 Uniform expensive—some pupils can't afford it; no money for own clothes.
4 Everyone's different—uniform can't hide this. Need to learn to accept differences. Children in other countries don't wear uniform.

b Make Miss Clark's speech in reply, using the notes below. Begin:
'Mr Chairman, on behalf of the staff, I wish to oppose the motion that school uniform should be abolished...
1 Everyone's the same—all people and all pupils of the school; uniform helps to show this equality. Shows where pupils belong.
2 School not the place for fashion shows—if wear own clothes rich and pretty girls show off. Pupils look at clothes instead of blackboard, books.
3 Some parents can't afford lots of new clothes—uniform cheaper; doesn't change like fashion—can be passed on.
4 Agree that the present uniform *is* ugly—suggest we appoint a sub-committee to design a more modern uniform.

c Add comments from the floor and take a vote.

C For further discussion
1 Do you wear school uniform? If so, describe it. If not, design one.
2 In what ways are people different from each other? Can uniform hide differences between school children? Should it?
3 Which people in the following list wear uniform at work? Can you suggest why they do/don't? Bank clerks, lawyers, teachers, businessmen, policemen, nurses, housewives, shop assistants, secretaries, soldiers.
4 Who makes the decisions in the following groups? Can you suggest why?—in a football team/in an aeroplane/in a factory/in a hospital/in a school?

D Draw up an agenda for a meeting of an Entertainments Sub-Committee which is planning a school concert.

22 The young scientist: cruel or curious?

There was once a schoolboy who was very interested in spiders. Two things puzzled him. Spiders didn't seem to have any ears, and they had a lot of legs. One day he had an idea. Spiders must have extra legs so that they can hear. He discussed this idea with his biology teacher.

'That's an interesting theory,' said the teacher, 'but you must think of an experiment to prove it.' So the boy did.

> **Experiment:** to see if spiders hear with their legs
>
> **Apparatus:** sharp knife, spider, table.
>
> **Method:** (i) The spider was put in the middle of the table. It was told to jump.
>
> **Result:** (i) It jumped.
>
> **Method:** (ii) The spider's legs were cut off. It was put back on the table. It was told to jump.
>
> **Result:** (ii) It failed to jump.
>
> ---
>
> **Conclusion:** The spider did not jump because it could not hear the instruction.
>
> ∴ Spiders hear with their legs.

Did he prove his theory? Is *one* experiment enough to prove anything?

The young scientist: cruel or curious?

Presentation 2 **22**

A Comprehension
1 Who was once very interested in spiders? What puzzled him?
2 What idea did he have?
3 Who did he discuss it with?
4 What did he tell the boy to do?
5 What was the aim of the boy's experiment?
6 What apparatus did he use?
7 Describe the two parts of the experiment:—the method and the results.
8 What conclusion did the boy draw from his experiment?
9 What did he prove, if anything?
10 Do you think the spider felt pain?
11 Was the boy cruel or curious?

B Should scientists experiment on living creatures?

a State the case FOR
1 Must do experiments—can't find out facts any other way.
Help us learn about life—how muscles, ears, eyes work.
2 Interesting—more knowledge.
Useful—helps us fight disease; find causes, cures.
Test new drugs etc. on animals—can't risk killing people.
3 Treat animals well—better than many pets: clean cages, good food etc.
Use animals no one wants; breed some specially.

b State the case AGAINST
1 All creatures feel pain—wrong to breed animals to suffer. Scientists cruel—like small boys who pull wings off flies.
2 Already know about life—no need for more experiments.
Students can look up facts.
More important to be kind than curious.
3 Scientists selfish—should do experiments on themselves.
Wrong to use animals to cure human diseases—find volunteers.

C For further discussion
1 Do you do experiments at school? If so, what do you learn from them?
2 Why do people keep pets? How do they treat them?
3 The following creatures are used in scientific experiments:—insects, frogs, mice, rabbits, guinea pigs, cats, dogs, monkeys, horses. Do you think some suffer more than others? Are scientists cruel? Should they use human volunteers instead? Could they?
4 Which is more important, to be kind to animals or to cure human diseases?
5 What do you know about these diseases: —smallpox, malaria, cancer, polio, tuberculosis? What causes them? Can they be cured, or prevented? How?

D Would you volunteer? Why/why not?

WANTED

HUMAN GUINEA PIGS

come and catch a cold!

help scientists find a cure

Comfortable rooms, free food AND pocket-money

Apply to: Common Cold Unit, Salisbury, England

FORUM
What should schools teach?

Editor This month our panel looks at education. Everyone seems to want more schools. But what *sort* of schools do we want?

Politician Good ones, of course. My party believes that good schools make good citizens.

Headmaster I prefer to talk of good *people*. In my school we aim to develop character. We try to teach the pupils about right and wrong, and...

Mrs Barnes But that's the family's job! Schools should prepare children for their future careers.

Mr Barnes I agree. Teach useful subjects and help the pupils pass exams.

Businessman We'd be happy in my firm if schools taught their pupils to read, write and count properly! But teachers don't seem to care about the needs of industry.

Headmaster Work's only part of life. We feel we must educate children for leisure too. I'd like more art, music and games on the timetable.

Professor There's too much already. What about academic work? Schools should pass on knowledge from one generation to another.

Editor Well, *we* can't agree. What does the younger generation think?

Professor

Politician

Headmaster

Mr Barnes

Mrs Barnes

Businessman

What should schools teach?

Presentation 1 **23**

A Comprehension
1 What's the subject of the forum?
2 Do people agree about the sort of schools they want?
3 How many points of view are stated?
4 What does the politician believe?
5 How does the headmaster differ?
6 Why does Mrs Barnes disagree?
7 What does her husband think?
8 Is the businessman satisfied with the work of schools? Why/why not?
9 What would the headmaster like on the timetable? Why?
10 Who disagrees with him? Why?
11 Can you suggest why the members of the panel disagree so much?
12 Who do *you* agree with most? Why?

B What should schools teach?
Summarise the viewpoint of each member of the panel.

1 The Politician: wants good schools—teach pupils to be good citizens.

2 The Headmaster: (a) wants good people—his school aims to develop character; teach about right and wrong. (b) educate for leisure—work only part of life; more art, music, games on the timetable.

3 Mr and Mrs Barnes: family's job to teach right and wrong. Schools—prepare children for future careers; teach useful subjects; help pupils pass exams.

4 The Businessman: firm wants people who can read, write etc. Schools don't teach basic skills properly—teachers don't care about needs of industry.

5 The Professor: wants more academic work—too much art, music etc. Schools—pass on knowledge from one generation to next.

C For further discussion
1 How would you describe (a) a good citizen (b) a good person?
2 How have you learnt about right and wrong? Who should teach morals?
3 Which school subjects do you think are the most useful? Why?
4 In what ways can schools prepare their pupils for their future careers?
5 Who taught you to read, write and count? Could people learn these basic skills if there were no schools? Why/why not?
6 Is it true that teachers don't care about industry's needs? If so, why?
7 Do you think people need to be educated for leisure? Why/why not?
8 What do *you* think schools should teach? What can they best teach?
9 At what age should pupils leave school? When does *education* end?

D Plan a timetable:
i Make a list of subjects you'd like to learn. Say why.
ii Allow 35 lesson-periods in a week. How much time will you give each subject?
iii Plan a timetable to suit one of the members of the panel.

24 Equal rights?

The Bell Family Charter

Housework <u>All</u> members of the family must do an equal share of the housework according to age and ability. A list of duties will be put up each week.

Free time Children and parents have an equal right to free time.

Visitors Children have a right to bring friends home whenever they like.

Bedtime Bedtime shall be fixed according to age. Over 15's may go to bed when they like.

Rules for parents Parents must not break promises.
Parents must not cancel arrangements suddenly.
Parents must not criticize their children in public.

NB Parents are not always right!

Signed:
Martin Bell (Father, engineer)
Elizabeth Bell (Mother, 3rd Grade teacher)
John Bell (Aged 16, at High School)
Kate Bell (Aged 14, at High School)
Andrew Bell (Aged 6, in 1st Grade)

Equal rights?

Presentation 2 **24**

A What are the facts?
1. How many people are there in the Bell family?
2. What nationality are they? How do you know?
3. Who's the youngest?
4. What are the parents' jobs?
5. Do the children all go to school?
6. How is the housework divided?
7. How does each member of the family know which job to do?
8. Who gets the most free time?
9. How often can the children bring visitors home?
10. Can Andrew go to bed when he likes? Explain the rules about bedtime.
11. What are the rules for parents?
12. Do the children think their parents never make mistakes?
13. Do the parents and children have equal rights? Why/why not?

B What does the charter imply?
a Do you agree or disagree with the following statements? What are the arguments FOR and AGAINST each one?
1. Husbands should help their wives with the housework.
2. Married women have the right to go out to work.
3. Boys should do as much housework as girls.
4. Small children should be given jobs to do.
5. Children need as much free time as adults, and should be given it.
6. Children's friends are as important as their parents' friends.
7. Children over 15 are sensible enough to fix their own bedtime.
8. Parents must not do anything to upset their children.

C What about your family?
1. Do you have any rules in your family? Who made them? What are they?
2. Who does the housework in your family? Do you help? Why/why not?
3. Who gets the most free time in your family? Why? What do your parents do in their free time? How do you and your friends spend your free time?
4. What happens about visitors in your family? How do you entertain them?
5. What time do you go to bed? What about the other members of the family?
6. Do your parents ever criticise you? What for? Are they right?

D Talking points
1. Why do people break promises and cancel arrangements suddenly? Have you ever had to? Is it always wrong to do so? Why/why not?
2. What duties do parents have that children don't?
3. How will you bring up your own children?
4. Has family life changed in the last 50 years? If so, how? Tell us what you know of family life in the past, and in other countries today.

E Duty list:
Can you work out a list of duties that would give an equal share of the housework to each member of the Bell family?

25 Motor vehicles – *a blessing or a curse?*

a   Picnic

b   Traffic jam

c   Fire!

d   Car crash

49

Motor vehicles—a blessing or a curse?

Presentation 2

25

A Look at the photos
a Picnic
1. Describe the man and the woman.
2. Are they staying in a hotel?
3. How did they get to their picnic place?

b Traffic jam
1. How fast is the traffic moving?
2. Which of the following vehicles can you see:—cars, taxis, buses, lorries, vans, bicycles?
3. Where was the photo taken? Have you any idea?
4. What time of day could it be?

c Fire!
1. Does the photo show a fire engine or an ambulance?
2. Can you see a policeman or a fireman?
3. What's he doing?

d Car crash
1. How many vehicles can you see?
2. How many people can you see?
3. Has a car or a lorry crashed?
4. Can it be driven away? Why/why not?
5. Is it summer or winter? Say why.
6. What do you think happened?

B Motor vehicles—a blessing or a curse?
a State the blessings.
1. Bring freedom—can travel further, faster; lorries, vans carry goods from door to door; cars comfortable.
2. Bring help quickly—police, fire engines, ambulances.
   Give us good postal services.
3. Nice to own a car—can visit our friends easily, go on picnics, go to the country from towns.
4. Driving is fun—motor racing.

b State the curses.
1. Spoil our cities—danger, noise; traffic jams—can't move.
   Poison the air—use up oxygen, give out lead, carbon monoxide.
2. Spoil the countryside—heavy lorries; take land for roads; old cars left in fields.
3. Cars—expensive, ugly, unhealthy; better to walk, ride a bicycle.
4. Driving is dangerous—crashes.

C What's your opinion?
1. Do you think motor vehicles have improved life or not? Give your reasons.
2. Which do you think is the best way to travel:—by car, by train, on a bicycle, or on foot? Say why.
3. Do you think cars are beautiful or ugly? What about other motor vehicles?
4. Do you think motor vehicles spoil the countryside? Why/why not?
5. Can you suggest how to stop (i) motor accidents (ii) traffic jams?

D Talking points
1. Does your family own a car? If so, what do you use it for?
2. Have you ever seen a motor accident/fire? Describe what happened.
3. Would you like to be a policeman or ambulance driver? Give your reasons.

E Choose a car
Put the following points in order:—(a) good brakes (b) fast (c) comfortable (d) easy to park (e) smart appearance (f) cheap to run.

26

Foolish or *fashionable?*

Susan Oh Dad. I've been invited to a party on Saturday.

Mr Brown How nice. Where is it?

Susan At the Winters' house. They're very rich, so I'll need a new dress.

Mr Brown What's wrong with your pretty blue one? You've only worn it twice.

Susan I've had it for *ages*. Everyone's seen it.

Mr Brown Well, they'll have to see it again. I can't afford to buy new dresses for you every month. I'm not made of money.

Susan But Dad, a dress only costs a few pounds.

Mr Brown Really Susan. What *do* you learn at school? Hundreds of girls never get any new clothes. And in many parts of the world your weekly pocket-money would have to feed a whole family.

Susan I don't care.

Mr Brown Well, I do. You're getting very selfish, and you're foolish about money. That's why I'm not going to buy you a new dress. I'll give the money to charity instead.

Foolish or fashionable?

Presentation 1 **26**

A Comprehension
1 What had Susan been invited to?
2 Why does she want a new dress?
3 What does her father think she should wear?
4 Why does Susan disagree?
5 Why can't her father afford to buy new dresses every month?
6 Does Susan think dresses are cheap or expensive?
7 How much does she know about life in poorer families?
8 Why does her father say she's foolish about money?
9 Why does he think she's selfish?

B Two points of view.
a State Susan's point of view.
1 Need a new dress—party at Winters' house—very rich. Everyone's seen blue dress—no longer fashionable.
2 Father doesn't understand. Could easily afford a new dress—costs a few pounds.
3 Talks of other girls—no new clothes; other countries—no money for food. I don't care—can't help them.

b State Mr Brown's point of view.
1 Susan wants a new dress—party with rich friends BUT has a pretty blue dress, worn twice. She can wear it again.
2 Can't buy new dresses every month. Susan's foolish about money—talks of a few pounds.
3 She's ignorant, selfish—many girls never get new clothes; pocket-money would feed a family. Give money to charity, not Susan.

C What's your opinion?
1 Do you think Susan needs a new dress? Why/why not?
2 If her father *can* afford to buy her a new dress, should he refuse?
3 Why do hundreds of girls never get any new clothes? Do *you* care?
4 How much pocket-money do you think Susan gets? Would she save any?
5 Do you think Susan is selfish? Why/why not? Can her father make her care about poorer people? Did he do the right thing?

D Talking points
1 What clothes are fashionable at present? Do you think women and girls are too interested in fashion? What about men and boys?
2 What do you think is a fair amount of pocket-money? Do girls need more than boys? Should older children get more than younger ones?
3 Should children give money to charity? Talk about a charity you know.
4 Why are some countries/families richer than others? Can anything be done about it? What do *you* think should be done?

E A proverb: 'Charity begins at home.' Do you agree?

27 What kind of mind have you got?

Psychologists study our minds and try to find out how we think. They have discovered that people have different mental abilities. Some people are good at solving problems about words: they have good verbal ability. Others are better at problems about numbers or shapes: they have good non-verbal ability. A few people are very good at all three kinds of problem: they are highly intelligent. Psychologists have also found that people can be divided into two main groups. The first group is good at finding the right answers to problems. The second group can think of many different answers to questions. What are your abilities? What kind of mind have you got? Here is a short test to help you find out. Write your answers on a piece of paper and do the test as quickly as you can.

A Find the right answer to these problems

Problems about shapes
1 One shape is unlike the others. Which is it?
   (i) (ii) (iii) (iv) (v)

Problems about numbers
One number is unlike the others. Which is it?
3 5 7 8 11

Problems about words
One word is unlike the others. Which is it?
bed   table   chair   fork   desk

2 Which shape should come in the middle?
(i) ··· (ii) · (iii) ∴
(iv) ·· (v) ∴

Which number should come in the middle?
3924   3492   3942   3429   3294

Which word should come in the middle?
house   country   town   district   street

3 Complete the following
☐ is to ⊘ as ◩
is to (i) ⊠ (ii) ◪
(iii) ⊘ (iv) ⊟ (v) ⊠

Complete the following
5 is to 25 as
7 is to 14 17 21 28 35

Complete the following
Flower is to rose as tree is to forest, oak, green, trunk, red.

B How many answers can you find to these questions?

4 How many uses can you suggest for the following objects?
   a a box   *b* a brick   *c* a blanket

5 Here are four statements. Which one interests you most? What do *you* think about it?
   a If you send boys and girls to the same schools they won't respect each other.
   b Money is the most important thing in the world.
   c 'No horse has two tails
      Every horse has one more tail than no horse
      Therefore every horse has three tails.'
   d The happiest years of your life are spent at school.

[Answers: see page 61]

What kind of mind have you got?

Presentation 2

27

A Questions on the test
1. What was your score for Nos 1–3?
2. Which groups did you do best:— problems about shapes, numbers or words?
3. How many answers did you think of for No 4? What were they?
4. Did you have any ideas on No 5? Tell us about them.
5. Did you do better in Section A or Section B? What kind of mind have *you* got?
6. Which problems should mathematicians do well? Why?
7. Which subject(s) should people who scored full marks in problems about words be good at?

B What kind of pupil are you?
Some psychologists think pupils can be divided into two types.

a *Describe Type 1*		b *Describe Type 2*
Poor on 1–3, good at 4, 5	Test scores	High on 1–3, low in 4, 5
Verbal	Type of ability	Non-verbal
Low	Accuracy	High
Wide, fluent	Vocabulary	Below average
History, English, Art	Best subjects	Physics, Maths, Chemistry.
Maths, Science	Worst subjects	English, History
Excellent	General Knowledge	Poor
Literature, Art	Interests	Making models, radio
To be a journalist	Ambition	To be an engineer

C What about you?
1. In which subjects is it important to be accurate? How accurate are you?
2. Which are your best/worst subjects? Why are you good/bad at them?
3. How good is your general knowledge? What about your vocabulary?
4. Which type of pupil do you think you are? What about your friends?

D Talking points
1. Tell us about your interests and ambitions.
2. Which do you think is most important for success at school: a good memory, high intelligence, hard work, imagination?
3. Which of the following people need to have a lot of new ideas at work: lawyers, composers, librarians, research scientists, engineers?
4. Are the following statements true? How could you find out?
   People are more intelligent at fifteen than at fifty.
   Boys are more intelligent than girls.

E Test your friends.
Make up a quiz of 10 questions to test your friends' General Knowledge
Here is the first question: 1 Which is the longest river in the world?

28 Focus on work

'An army marches on its stomach,' said Napoleon. The great general realised that people can't work when they're hungry: they haven't any energy. So he tried to give his soldiers plenty to eat. Our knowledge has advanced since then. Scientists can now measure the amount of energy that different kinds of food provide.* They can also calculate how much food different people require. How much food do *you* need? That depends partly on your sex, age and size, and partly on the work that you do. The harder you work, the more food you need. What kind of work requires the most energy? Scientists have studied this too. Look at the following chart. You'll soon see who works the hardest!

Daily calorie requirements

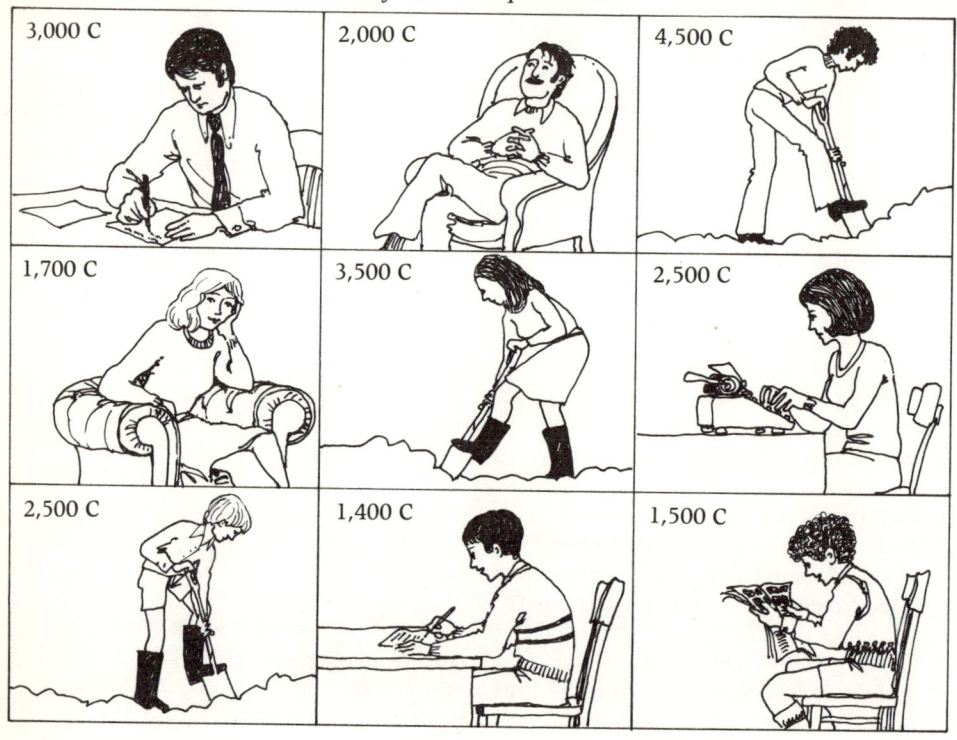

3,000 C	2,000 C	4,500 C
1,700 C	3,500 C	2,500 C
2,500 C	1,400 C	1,500 C

*They use a unit called a Calorie. 1 Calorie (1C)=1,000 calories. 1 calorie (1c)=the amount of heat needed to raise the temperature of 1 gram of water by 1° centigrade.

Focus on work

Presentation 2 **28**

A Comprehension
1 Who was Napoleon? Why did he give his soldiers plenty to eat?
2 What can scientists now measure?
3 What can they calculate?
4 What does the amount of food a person needs depend on?
5 What else have scientists studied?
6 What is the title of the chart?
7 How many calories a day does the man writing require?
8 Which man needs the most calories?
9 Which woman needs the least? Why?
10 What about the children? Which activity is the most energetic?
11 Would you expect writing or typing to use more energy? Why?
12 Why does the man writing need more calories than the woman typing?
13 Who needs the most calories when digging? Why?
14 Which of the activities shown are mental and which are physical?

B Are the following statements TRUE or FALSE? Give your reasons.
1 The chart tells us how many calories you need to do different jobs.
2 The chart shows that children don't work as hard as adults.
3 The chart proves that physical work is harder than mental work.
4 The chart shows that men, women and children need different amounts of food.
5 The chart shows that some activities use more energy than others.
6 The chart proves that men work harder than women.
7 The chart shows that calorie requirements are highest for people who use their muscles in their jobs.
8 The chart shows that it's easier to measure physical work than mental work.
9 The chart explains why fat people go on a diet and do exercises.

C What's your opinion?
1 What do *you* think work is? Is it what you are paid to do? Is it what you spend most time doing? Or what is it?
2 Why, if you use energy to play football, isn't football work? Or is it?
3 What sort of work can machines do for us? Have they improved life?
4 Do you learn Physics? What do physicists mean by work?
5 Do you think scientists *can* measure work? Why/why not?
6 Would *you* rather work with your muscles or with your mind? Why?
7 Would people be happier if they didn't have to work? Why/why not?

D Argue FOR and AGAINST the following statements:
1 Women should get equal pay for equal work.
2 People who do heavy manual work should be paid more than office workers.

E A quotation from Mencius, a Chinese philosopher of the 4th century B.C.
'There are those who use their minds and there are those who use their muscles. The former rule; the latter are ruled.' Has the world changed?

29 Examinations are a necessary evil

David is talking to his younger sister, Emma

Emma Hello David. What was the English exam like?

David All right. The examiners tried to be funny. Look at the first question.

>   **University of Newton**
>   General Certificate of Education
>   *Examination Summer 1972*
>
>   **English Language Ordinary Level**
>
>   *Time allowed:* 2½ hours
>   Answer all sections of this paper
>   *Section A:* Composition
>   Choose one of the following subjects:
>   1 'Examinations are a necessary evil'. *Discuss*
>   2 Should dangerous sports be abolished?

Emma Did you do it?

David Yes, I did actually. I could think of plenty to say about the evils of exams! I haven't slept properly for weeks.

Emma But the question suggests that they're necessary too. What did you say about that?

David Oh, I thought up a few points. Here, look at my notes. They're on the back.

Emma Is that all? You could have said lots more. Why didn't you suggest an alternative to exams?

David Listen, my clever little sister. As soon as you enter the exam room your mind goes blank. Wait till it's your turn! Anyway, let's not talk about it any more. I've got to revise two years' history before tomorrow.

> **EXAMS**
>
> *Necessary (pros)*
> make you work
> help you get jobs
>
> *Evil (cons)*
> divide people into pass or fail
> can't do your best — nerves

Examinations are a necessary evil

Presentation 2 **29**

A Comprehension
1 What was David telling Emma about?
2 What did he think of the paper?
3 Which composition subject did he choose? Why?
4 What did Emma notice about the question?
5 Did she think David had made plenty of points or only a few?
6 What did she think he ought to have suggested?
7 What was David's excuse?
8 Why did he change the subject?

B Are examinations a necessary evil?

a State the PROS of exams.
1 Necessary—make you work; show who's clever, stupid—help select people for jobs, university.
2 Fair—same time, questions for all. Public exams—no names, marked by strangers—what you know, not who you know for jobs etc.
3 Preparation for life—need ability to think quickly, a good memory. Do well in exams—succeed in life.

b State the CONS of exams.
1 Evil—test memory, not how much pupils understand; learn facts. Can't do your best—nerves etc.
2 Unfair—some people can't write quickly; 2 years' work in $1\frac{1}{2}$ hours. Examiners don't see best work—chance in life depends on 1 day.
3 Divide people—passes, fails. In life we need ability to work steadily, and to help others.

C For further discussion
1 What do *you* think of exams? Would you like to abolish them? Why/why not? If you didn't have exams do you think you would work harder or not? How might your lessons change? What do your parents/teachers think of exams?
2 What advice would you give to a friend before an important examination?
3 How do *you* think people should be selected for jobs, universities etc.?
4 What kinds of tests do people have to face in life outside school? Is it true that people who do well in exams succeed in later life? If so, why?
5 Is there an alternative to exams? Here are some suggestions. What are the pros and cons of each one?
   a Tests every month in each subject, but no yearly exams.
   b Keep a list of marks for the last three years at school.
   c Give pupils marks for character.
   d Give every pupil a certificate: e.g. X attended this school for 5 years. He worked well.
   e Keep examples of school work to show employers, universities.

D Why not improve exams?
Here is one idea: 'Allow pupils to take their notes into the examination so that they can show understanding rather than memory.' Do you agree? Can you suggest other ideas?

Viewpoint

SEPTEMBER

Sun	1	8
Mon	2	9

AUGUST

Sun	4	11	18	25
	5	12	19	26
	6	13	20	27
	7	14	21	28
1	8	15	22	29
2	9	16	23	30
3	10	17	24	31

JULY

Sun		7	14	21	28
Mon	1	8	15	22	29
Tues	2	9	16	23	30
Wed	3	10	17	24	31
Thurs	4	11	18	25	
Fri	5	12	19	26	
Sat	6	13	20	27	

The school holidays are too lon

says Mrs Pat Walker

Today the children of this country have at last returned to work. After two *months'* holiday pupils have started a new term. How many adults get such long holidays? Two to four weeks in the summer and public holidays—that's all the working man gets. As for the average woman, she's lucky to get a holiday at all. Children don't need such long holidays. In term-time they start work later and finish earlier than anyone else.

In the holidays most of them get bored, and some get into trouble. What a waste! If their overworked parents were given more free time instead, everyone would be happier.

This isn't just a national problem either—it's worldwide. Dates may be different from country to country, but the pattern's the same. Why should children do half as much work and get twice as much holiday as their parents?

The school holidays are too long

Presentation 1 **30**

A Comprehension
1 What's Mrs Walker complaining about?
2 When did she write her complaint?
3 Do children or adults get the longer holidays?
4 How much holiday does the working man get?
5 What about the average woman?
6 Why does Mrs Walker think children don't need long holidays?
7 Why does she want adults to have more free time?
8 What is the extent of the problem?
9 How do different countries compare?
10 What's Mrs Walker's final point?

B Are the school holidays too long?
a State Mrs Walker's argument.
1 School holidays too long—children—two months' holiday. Adults—man gets two, four weeks; woman—lucky to get a holiday.
2 Children don't need long holidays—term-time—start later, finish earlier; holidays—bored, trouble.
3 Waste—parents more free time, everyone happier. World problem—dates different, pattern same. Children half work, twice holiday.

b Construct a counter-argument.
1 Children need long holidays. Time to rest, play, visit relatives, places of interest; develop hobbies.
2 School hard work—learning new things all day; homework. Adults—men do same thing all day. Women stay at home, drink coffee. N.B. Children don't get paid.
3 Most children enjoy holidays. Mrs Walker jealous, tired. Remember—*teachers* need holidays.

C What's your opinion?
1 Do *you* think the school holidays are too long? Do you get bored? Say why.
2 Why do you think Mrs Walker felt so angry about the school holidays?
3 How much holiday does the average man get in this country? Is it enough? How does he spend it?
4 Can you suggest why some workers get longer holidays than others?
5 Do you agree that the average woman is lucky to get a holiday at all?
6 Who needs most holiday: men or women, children or adults? Give your reasons.
7 Why do different countries have different dates for school holidays?
8 Do you think your parents need more free time? Would it make them happier?
9 Do you think teachers need more holiday than other adults? Why/why not?

D Talking points
1 What did you do during the last school holidays? What are you planning to do for your next holiday? Describe the best holiday you've ever had.
2 Is it easy to plan a holiday to suit all the members of a family? Why?
3 When are the public holidays in this country? How do people spend them?

E A saying:
'A change is as good as a rest.' Is it?
Have a good holiday!

Answer page

1 Exercise C.
   a 4   b 3   c 2   d 1   e 0
   Total: 16–20 very good, 11–15 good, 6–10 could do better, 0–5 will have to try hard.

6 Exercise E.
   1c   2d   3d

8 Exercise E.
   1 Hydrogen and oxygen. (H_2O).   2 About half.
   3 a (ii)   b (i)   c (iii)

12 There is no market in High Wick on Wednesdays, so Bates couldn't have bought the flowers there. He could have taken the A 246 from Burton to West Cross and then the A 7 to Camford and Newton.

27
A	Shapes	Numbers	Words
1	ii	8	fork
2	i	3492	town
3	i	35	oak

Some useful phrases

A Expressing a personal viewpoint

1 In my opinion/view...
2 Personally, I think...
3 I'd say that...
4 In my experience...
5 As far as I'm concerned...
6 Speaking for myself...
7 I'd suggest that...
8 I'd like to point out that...
9 I believe that...
10 What I mean is that...

B Agreeing with another's viewpoint

1 Quite.
2 Exactly.
3 Yes, I agree.
4 That's true.
5 So do I/Neither do I.
6 I think so, too.
7 You're (absolutely) right.
8 I agree with you entirely.
9 That's a good point.
10 I go along with that.

C Disagreeing with another's viewpoint

1 However...
2 On the other hand...
3 On the contrary...
4 I don't agree with you.
5 I'm afraid I must disagree.
6 I'm sorry to disagree with you, but...
7 That's not (entirely) true.
8 Yes, but don't you think...
9 That's rather different.
10 That's not the same thing at all.

Also by LG Alexander

Language Practice Books:
Sixty Steps to Précis
Poetry and Prose Appreciation for Overseas Students
Essay and Letter-writing
A First Book in Comprehension, Précis and Composition
Question and Answer: Graded Aural/Oral Exercises
Reading and Writing English
Guided Composition in English Language Teaching

The Carters of Greenwood (Cineloops):
Teacher's Handbook
Elementary Workbook
Intermediate Workbook

Look, Listen and Learn:
Pupils' Books 1–4
Teacher's Books 1–4
Workbooks-Link Readers

New Concept English:
First Things First
Practice and Progress
Developing Skills
Fluency in English

Target 1–3
Pupils' and Teacher's Books

Longman Structural Readers, Stage 1:
Detectives from Scotland Yard
Car Thieves
Mr Punch

Longman Structural Readers, Stage 2:
April Fools' Day
Worth a Fortune
Professor Boffin's Umbrella
K's First Case

Longman Structural Readers, Stage 3:
Operation Mastermind
Good morning, Mexico!

Longman Integrated Comprehension and Composition Series:
General Editor

Tell Us a Story

Mainline

Uniform with this Volume:
For and Against:
An Oral Practice Book for Advanced Students of English